kid
V · I · D

FUN-DAMENTALS

OF VIDEO

INSTRUCTION

STAND-BY   SPEED-UP   READY

KAYE BLACK

WITH ILLUSTRATIONS BY
GORDON MURRAY

ZEPHYR PRESS
Tucson, Arizona

© 1989, **Zephyr Press,** Tucson, AZ

ISBN: 0-913705-44-6

Editor: Susan Newcomer
Designer: Kathleen Koopman

ACKNOWLEDGMENT
Thanks to Jo Taylor, Process Video Producer, for her expertise and guidance.

Zephyr Press, P.O. Box 66006, Tucson, Arizona 85728-6006

kid
V · I · D

FUN-DAMENTALS
_____
OF VIDEO
_____
INSTRUCTION

CONTENTS

INTRODUCTION 6

THE BASICS

    What Is Video? 8

    Basic Equipment

        Camera 9

        Video Cassette Recorder (VCR) 10

        Tripod 11

        Dolly 11

        Microphone 14

        Lights 14

        Television/Monitor 15

PRODUCTION TECHNIQUES

    The Camera

        Shots 16

        Framing the Shot 18

        Movement 19

        Transitions 20

    Choice of Video Treatment 22

    Lighting 23

    White Balancing 24

    Sound 24

    Graphics 25

    Production Cues and Gestures 26

    Editing 27

    Audio Dubbing 29

    Video Crew 30

    Hints and Cautions 32

VIDEO PRODUCTION IN 9 EASY LESSONS

Lesson 1   What Makes an Effective Production? 34

Lesson 2   The Mechanics: Simple Scripts and Storyboards 38

Lesson 3   Introducing Equipment: Producing a Simple Interview ...42

Lesson 4   Selecting a Program Treatment.....................................46

Lesson 5   Production: Technique, Terminology, Technicians 50

Lesson 6   Finalizing the Video Production Proposal......................54

Lesson 7   The Production! 58

Lesson 8   Logging and Editing Rough Footage 62

Lesson 9   Evaluation, Student-style 66

APPENDIX

Ways to Use Video in Schools 72

Optional Lesson: Process Video 74

Video Production Proposal 78

Suggestions for Positive Feedback...80

Materials for the Classroom 81

Sample Script and Storyboard Sheets......................................82

Blank Forms 85

Student Skill Chart...89

Glossary 91

References 95

INTRODUCTION

So you want to teach video?

So you want to teach your students to "convert audio and video signals into electronic pulses and record these pulses on electromagnetic tape"? Sounds technical, doesn't it? But is it? Does video have to be technical? Not at all!

Video is used everywhere—at home, in the office, in police departments, theaters, hospitals, banks, stores, libraries, restaurants—even schools! Anything people want to investigate, teach, or recall is, or soon will be, videotaped. Video is a part of the present that will affect the future in ways we haven't even imagined. What possibilities! You can prepare students for this future by getting involved in video now. Video is creative, challenging, and definitely fun! And it can be extremely useful in the daily life of your school.

I started teaching video like most teachers—I knew nothing! I even resisted doing video because I felt "technophobic." But when I thought about the impact that video will have on students and their futures, I realized that the advantages of doing video far outweigh the disadvantages. So I decided to do video *for them*. And— surprise! We learned together. I learned that teaching video can be fun. By the end of the unit, I was doing video *for me!*

You can teach video to your class, too. With some basic equipment and this guide, you can begin to enjoy and use this important medium.

KIDVID presents a practical learning program to help students understand and use video. They will be doing the writing, the camerawork, the editing. You will simply supervise. The curriculum is designed to be used with upper-elementary school students, but with a little revision, the curriculum can be used with just about any age level.

Specifically, **KIDVID** will help students:

- recognize the elements that affect the quality of a video production,
- develop the analytical skills necessary to interpret relationships among these elements,
- construct criteria for evaluating effective video productions, and
- learn the fundamental techniques of video production, including preproduction planning (using scripts and storyboards) and technical skills (working with the camera and lights, for example). In **KIDVID**, students move quickly from theory to "hands-on" experience with equipment, and, for them, "hands-on" is the most exciting part.

KIDVID is organized into three parts. **The Basics** presents a general introduction to video and basic video equipment. **Production Techniques** introduces the basic skills and terminology you will need to teach video. **Video Production in 9 Easy Lessons** presents a step-by-step guide for teaching video production, from Lesson 1, which invites students to evaluate their favorite television show, to Lesson 9, which asks students to evaluate the video production they have just completed in class! In addition, the appendix includes a glossary of technical terms, sample forms, a list of references, material on the many uses of video in the schools, and information on how to prepare instructional material for the classroom.

If you didn't think video was easy before **KIDVID**, you will now! So let's begin . . . 5 . . . 4 . . .3 . . .2 . . . 1 . . . Roll the tape!

THE BASICS

What Is Video?

Basic Equipment

    Camera

    Video Cassette Recorder

        (VCR)

    Tripod

    Dolly

    Microphone

    Lights

    Television/Monitor

Video /'vid-e-o/ n., adj., [L *videre* to see + E -o] 1. Relating to or used in the transmission or reception of the television image.

video, Latin, *I see*

Webster's Seventh New Collegiate Dictionary (Springfield, Mass.: G. & C. Merriam Company, Publishers, 1963).

WHAT IS VIDEO?

Videotape is a thin plastic film covered with a magnetically sensitive coating. Audio and video information is recorded in separate sections (called "tracks") on the tape. When the tape is recording, audio and video signals are converted to electrical impulses by the camera. These impulses are stored on the videotape as changes in the magnetic coating.

When we think of video we often think of television. Television has been around for almost fifty years (it was actually invented in the early 1900s but perfected much later). Video—the recording of the audio and video images—took longer to develop and is still evolving today.

The first videotape recorder was introduced in the late 1950s and was expensive, cumbersome, and fragile. Many different formats (methods of recording that are incompatible) were competing for the market at first, but finally the market condensed to two basic formats, Beta and VHS (which are still incompatible).

Videotape is *not* film. It does not look, feel, or act like film. Videotape has no frames or sprockets, and it does not need to be threaded, spliced, or touched in any way. It is cheaper than film and provides immediate feedback. It does not need to be developed in a laboratory. It can be stored, erased, and reused, sped up, slowed down, or even paused to "freeze" the action. It is easy to revise, edit, and correct. The picture quality of videotape will not deteriorate over time. It is *not* film.

With one or two pieces of equipment, video can be easily shown at home on a standard television set. No special camera or screen is necessary. A video cassette player (or recorder) hooked up to a television will show a variety of videotaped material, including purchased or rented movies, instructional tapes, tapes of the piano recital or school soccer game, and even video productions made at home or in the classroom!

In many cities, local cable companies have added public access channels to their broadcast formats. This simply means that individual citizens have

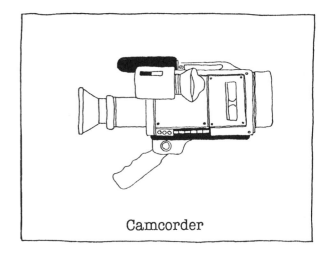

Camcorder

been granted access to three or four cable television channels to display their own video material. More and more individuals are making video productions. Many cities have set up community cable corporations to give citizens access to equipment, studios, and training. Contact your local television company to find which access options are available in your area.

Video prices continue to fall, both for equipment and supplies. Quality and reliability remain high, and special features that add fancy effects are being added to equipment or becoming standard more and more.

Video production is becoming easier every day. With a few pieces of equipment and an imaginative mind, anyone can make a video!

But you will need some basic equipment. This is outlined in the following section.

BASIC EQUIPMENT
Camera

A video camera translates light into recorded electronic information. Two types of video cameras are available:

- a camcorder, which records on a videotape inserted directly into the camera, and
- a separate camera that plugs into a video cassette recorder (VCR), where the recording takes place.

The VCR is usually portable, but it can also be a typical home or school tabletop model. Some VCRs need a special adaptor before a camera can be plugged into them for recording. Camcorders and portable VCRs usually require a battery pack for power.

Recording a videotape with a camcorder is relatively easy. The camera usually fits handily onto a person's shoulder. The cameraperson simply points the camera at the scene to be recorded and pushes a button. Recording with a VCR and separate camera often involves a team of people and several wires or cables. Although most educators are not in a position to choose which kind of camera to purchase, each set-up has advantages and disadvantages.

Camcorder

Advantages:
- can be operated by one person
- more convenient to use
- needs no cable connectors to VCR to record
- more portable, less cumbersome
- most new models have many automatic features (white balancing, focus, and so forth)

Disadvantages:
- when one part breaks, the entire camera is usually unusable
- can be heavy and awkward for students
- some models need a separate VCR and television for viewing tapes later in class

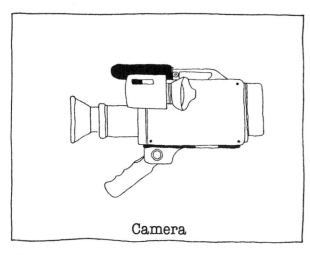

Camera

Camera and Separate VCR

Advantages:

- each part is usually less heavy than a camcorder
- the camera may have more recording features
- the VCR may have more recording features

Disadvantages:

- more cumbersome
- not portable unless plugged into a battery-operated, portable VCR
- more cables are needed for taping
- the camera team must synchronize their actions

THE BASICS

In deciding which camera to use, keep in mind how you will be using it.

The VCR and separate camera arrangement is impractical for working outdoors, for example, although it is perfectly suitable for recording school debates or assemblies.

Regardless of what camera you use, to use it correctly you will need to know all its parts. The generic camera illustrated on p.12 may differ from yours, *so be sure to refer to the owner's manual for specific directions.* This cannot be overemphasized! Before all else fails, read the directions!

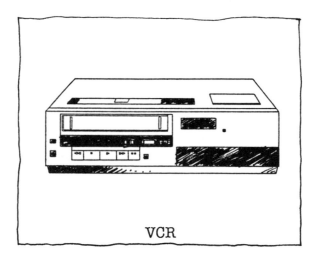

VCR

Video Cassette Recorder (VCR)

A video cassette recorder (VCR), also called a videotape recorder (VTR), records a signal onto a videotape and plays the tape back. If you use a camcorder you will not need a VCR for recording. You will be using the VCR only for playing back your recorded material. If you use a camera that must attach to a VCR for taping, you will need to take the VCR with you when you record. Unless the VCR has the right kind of input plug, you will also need the appropriate connection box to run from the camera to the VCR. (VCRs used in the home usually do not have a built-in camera plug, so they need the special connection box.) Portable VCRs used with a camera must be plugged into an electrical wall socket or attached to a special battery for power.

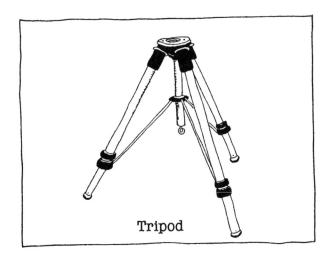

Tripod

greater movement, you can purchase a "video head" (also called a "fluid head" or "fluid effect head") that will allow you to move the camera smoothly in any direction. You may also purchase a single pole called a "monopod" that screws directly into the bottom of the camera—it doesn't use a head—to steady the camera.

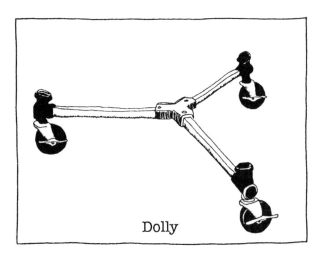

Dolly

Tripod

A tripod is a three-legged adjustable stand used to hold the camera steady during taping. It often comes with a special plate that screws into a universal slot in the bottom of the camera or camcorder. This plate allows you to attach or remove your camera from the tripod with the flip of a switch. The tripod can also be purchased with a "camera head" or "pan head," a top designed to hold a camera. With this head you can lock your camera in position securely, but you will have little freedom of movement. For

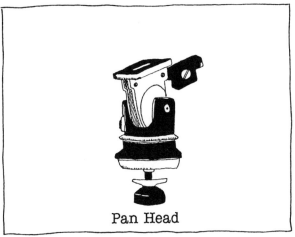

Pan Head

Dolly

A dolly is a wheeled rack to which a tripod can be attached. It allows the tripod and camera to be wheeled around smoothly.

Young students can use both tripods and dollies. Unfortunately, better tripods and dollies are more expensive, but the extra investment is worth it. Because young hands are not strong enough to properly tighten the connections, you'll appreciate a good tripod and dolly.

Parts of the Camcorder

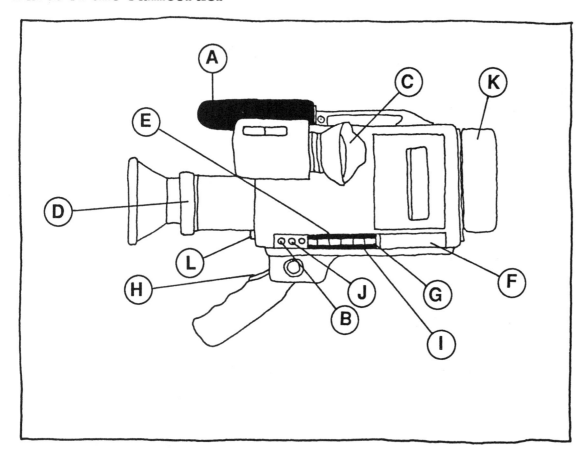

A. Microphone: Records sound on the tape. There may also be an input plug for another external mike.

B. White balance: This switch needs to be set when beginning to tape and adjusted when you change lighting (for example, when you move from inside to outside). White balancing tells the camera what "white" is. Some newer models may have an automatic white balance function, or claim to! It is best for you to adjust the balance manually if you can. See your camera manual for directions and "White Balancing" (p. 24).

C. Viewfinder: The viewfinder allows you to see what you are taping (most display in black and white, however), and, in some models, it lets you play back and review what you have taped. It also displays various indicators to tell you if you are recording, if the light is adequate, if the battery is charged, and other information. Check the manual to determine if the viewfinder sees what the camera sees or just what the viewfinder sees. This can make a big difference. You may aim the camera at something specific, for example, only to find that the object is off-center on your tape.

D. Lens assembly: The lens assembly handles all the light that comes into the camera. It is similar to a still camera in its construction. You can add special lenses to get special effects. This is the part of the camera that will focus and zoom.

E. Control panel: These controls enable you to use the camcorder as a VCR (rewind or play the tape back through the monitor, for example).

F. Special effects panel: These controls allow you to include special effects on your tape (the day, date, or time, for example).

G. Record button: The record button enables you to record and to pause during the recording.

H. Zoom toggle button: This two-way button enables you to zoom the camera lens in and out. It is sometimes marked "T" for telephoto and "W" for wide-angle.

I. Stand-by switch: When pressed, this switch places the camera in a stand-by mode. The camera will turn off most of its power to conserve the tape and battery. Some cameras automatically switch to stand-by when they are on but not recording for a period of time.

J. Back-light button: This button is used to improve the image when light comes from behind the subject, casting the subject into darkness.

K. Battery: Most batteries are rechargeable. You can purchase a larger battery that will supply power longer. Some "batteries" can also plug directly into a wall outlet. Batteries must be faithfully recharged after each use!

L. Focus: This button will switch the camera from automatic focus to manual focus. With manual focus, you must focus the lens yourself.

Microphone

Video cameras record sound as well as pictures. A microphone is often housed inside the camera, and in addition, most cameras have a separate input plug to which an external mike can be attached. Be aware that attaching an external mike will usually cancel the internal one. You must use the right size plug or "jack" to fit the input plug. Plug adaptors can usually be purchased off the shelf from a local electronics store.

Do not plan to use a separate microphone and tape recorder to record people talking because it is almost impossible to match lips and sound in a video production unless you have excellent editing equipment.

Lights

A camera simply will not work without light. Light is what is recorded electronically on the videotape. Two types of light are available: natural light and artificial light.

Natural light is an obvious choice for outdoors. Direct sunlight is a strong source, but overhead, it often casts harsh shadows, the shadows keep moving, and it may make your subjects squint. To compensate for these drawbacks, you can use reflectors or additional "fill" lights. Reflectors are white or shiny surfaces that bounce light back. They can be used to fill in shadows. Fill lights are simply electric lights that add additional lighting to the scene. Remember that they will need a source of power to work, either a battery or an outlet, and they must be strong or close enough to match the sunlight.

Artificial light can be as simple as a few clip-on "scoop" lights. Available at any hardware store, these inexpensive lights are fine for beginners, but be aware that these lights will not accept very high wattage (check the lamp, usually rated up to 100 watts). Similar but more heavy duty scoop lamps will accept up to 500-watt bulbs and can be purchased at any camera store. Do not forget the special tripods available to hold lights. A camera store can introduce you to a variety of other lights and lamps and teach you a lot more about lighting. Regular room lights, for example, tend to cast more of a yellow-orange tint than the camera can compensate for.

Television/Monitor

A television or a monitor must accompany your VCR so you can view your taped material. The difference between a television and a monitor is this: a standard television receives video and audio signals on a radio frequency through its antenna, whereas a monitor receives signals only through its input connections. Monitors usually accept signals from such sources as VCRs, video cameras, computers, and so forth. Monitors usually provide a better picture because there is no antenna interference, and video signals can be separated from audio signals, which is not true on most televisions. Some televisions can be used as monitors, however, so check carefully when you purchase equipment.

PRODUCTION TECHNIQUES

The Camera
   Shots
   Framing the Shot
   Movement
   Transitions
Choice of Video Treatment
Lighting
White Balancing
Sound
Graphics
Production Cues
   and Gestures
Editing
Audio Dubbing
Video Crew
Hints and Cautions

Long Shot

Close-up

THE CAMERA: SHOTS

Students should practice looking through the camera viewfinder and visualizing the shots they want to make. A variety of shots are possible, from a full frontal shot, in which the camera is aimed directly at the front of the subject, to a sideways shot or an over-the-shoulder shot. Each of these shots can be further refined according to how close the camera is to the subject, from a full-length shot to a close-up (and whether the lens has zoomed in or out). These refinements can be further divided into camera angle—

whether the camera is looking down on the subject or looking up at the subject.

Keep in mind that each kind of shot conveys a subtle message to the video audience. For example, an extreme close-up of a subject's face taken while the subject is talking would tend to heighten the dramatic quality of what the person is saying and focus on the person's internal qualities. Compare this with a full-length shot taken from below: the subject would appear distant and imposing.

Frontal Shots

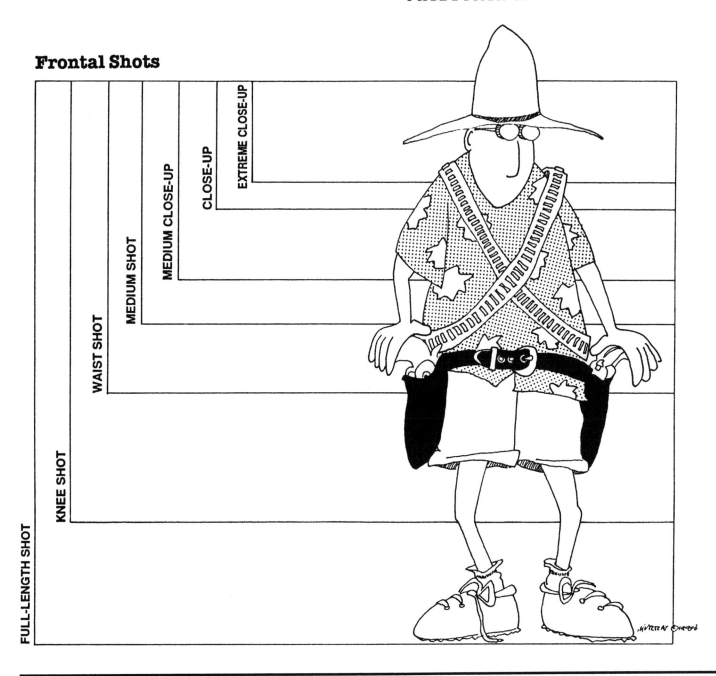

Choose your shots carefully, not only for their visual quality but also for the emotional impact they will have on the audience.

A   Less Visual Interest

B   More Visual Interest

C   With Thirds

D   With Talking Space

THE CAMERA: FRAMING THE SHOT

Once a kind of shot is selected (for example, medium close-up), have the cameraperson mentally divide the frame into thirds horizontally and vertically. The intersections of the lines are where the viewer tends to focus. With this in mind, a few hints will greatly improve your pictures:

- avoid the center of the frame (see illustration A, left); place your subject at one of the inter-sections for more visual interest (illustration B)
- keep the speaker's eyes about two-thirds from the bottom of the frame (illustration C)
- avoid cutting off subjects' heads when taping a group of people
- give the subject "talking space" or "looking room" (illustration D) on the screen—allow for extra space on the side toward which the subject is talking or looking. Failure to balance a shot in this way is a common error among novices.

When framing a shot, pay attention to how something looks through the

Dolly

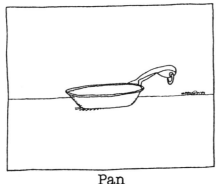

Pan

Truck

Tilt

viewfinder, not just how it looks in real life. Make sure the scene in the viewfinder is balanced. Encourage students to balance for color as well, remembering that bright colors draw attention, and busy backgrounds (those with a lot of detail or action) tend to overwhelm a subject. To change color imbalance, change the lighting or move the subject or camera for a new angle, lighting, or emphasis.

THE CAMERA: MOVEMENT

Once you begin taping, you will want to change the picture in the frame. A full minute of a single shot can be boring indeed! Several camera moves are available:

Zoom: When the camera lens zooms in or out, you are actually changing the focal length of the lens or the distance between the lens and the recording surface without moving the camera. Zooming in gives the appearance of moving in on the subject. Zooming out gives the appearance of moving out. This is accomplished smoothly by pressing the zoom toggle button on the camera—the "T" side of the button (for telephoto) allows you to zoom in and the "W" side (for wide-angle) allows you to zoom out. I tell students that if they have trouble remembering that "T" is for telephoto and "W" is for wide-angle, they should remember that "T" is for toward the subject and "W" is for a-Way from the subject.

This feature is the one most commonly misused by amateurs!

Dolly in or **out:** Used as a verb, to dolly means to physically move the whole camera toward or away from the subject. This is accomplished most smoothly when the camera is mounted on a steady object such as a tripod or dolly.

Pan: To pivot the camera from side to side. Most people tend to pan without knowing where they are panning to!

Truck: To physically move the camera left or right to follow the subject.

Tilt: To move the camera up or down.

THE CAMERA: TRANSITIONS

Many basic camera moves may also serve as transitions from one scene to another. As the subject moves, for example, you can pan or tilt to follow the action. To conclude a scene, you might want to zoom in on the subject's face or zoom out to a full-length shot of the subject standing. Transitions are done smoothly and well only with a lot of practice.

Each movement produces certain effects. Normally, for example, panning should be done slowly and smoothly so the video audience can easily follow the camera shot. Panning so quickly that the background becomes a blur, however, may assist you in changing from one scene to another. Each movement has its own challenges, so be sure to practice!

One final note: **Always point the camera lens away from the lights or the sun!** Direct light could permanently damage the lens.

Pan as transition

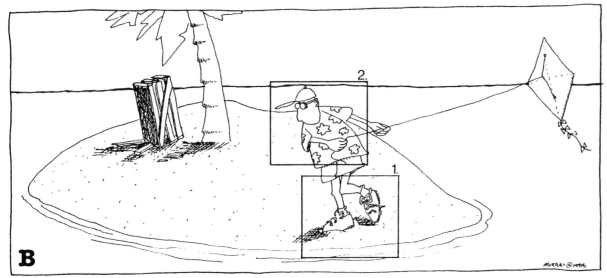

Tilt as transition

Zoom as transition

Two other transitions are also available:

- you can "iris down," that is, gradually close the iris of the lens to create a "fade." Note that the cameraperson must do this manually.
- you can quickly put black cardboard in front of the lens. (Do it quickly or it will look silly.)

Transitions

A. Pan as transition

Frame 1 to frame 3, pan left

Frame 3 to frame 1, pan right

B. Tilt as transition

Frame 1 to frame 2, tilt up

Frame 2 to frame 1, tilt down

C. Zoom as transition

Frame 1 to frame 2, zoom out

Frame 2 to frame 1, zoom in

CHOICE OF
VIDEO TREATMENT

Four basic types of video treatment are described at the right. There are more than these basic types, of course, and some video productions may combine types. When helping students plan a treatment for their video production, keep in mind that some subjects suggest certain treatments. A video production about the effects of divorce on children, for example, would be particularly dramatic, whereas a video production of a student council meeting would probably be simple documentary. By mixing treatments, however, or using a treatment seemingly unsuitable for the subject, students may produce interesting, creative results.

Note that the video productions described in the following nine lessons are studio productions, that is, students prepare a script and storyboard and other students act out parts in a controlled setting. An alternative to studio video is "process video," videotaping that records live, unre-

Educational videos demonstrate how something works, present factual information, or describe something.

Humorous videos are meant to make people laugh.

Documentary videos record for historical purposes some event or occurrence.

Dramatic videos are meant to dramatize some fictional or nonfictional story.

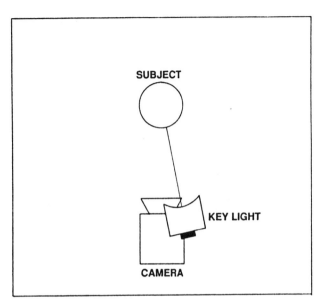

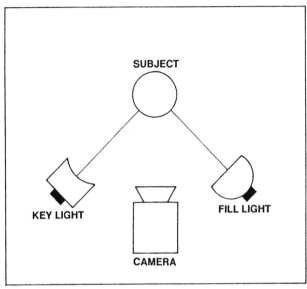

hearsed action. The uses for process video are myriad: to record artistic or athletic performances, to provide feedback for artistic or athletic training, or to monitor progress in a learning situation. Studio production is easier for beginning students because the setting is more controlled and basic video techniques play a greater role, but process video is an important aspect of video production. An optional lesson plan on process video is provided in the appendix on p. 74.

LIGHTING

You can light a set with only one light—called the key light—usually above the camera and off to one side. You can light a set with two lights: the key spot on one side and a smaller light—the fill light—off to the other side. Three lights give even better lighting: the key spot and the fill light as described above and a third light behind the subject, called a back light.

Special effects can be achieved with lighting from different angles—above,

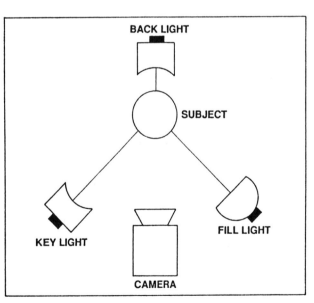

below, behind, to the side. Colored filters can also be used for effect, but use them carefully. Lights get hot!

If lights are too harsh, consider using a reflector or bouncing light off a white ceiling to diffuse the glare. Observe safety precautions at all times.

Remember, lighting is an art, a whole field in itself, so keep things simple at first until you get more experience. There is plenty of room to grow!

WHITE BALANCING

Your eyes and brain adjust automatically to changes in the color of light. A videocamera is not that flexible. Most cameras come with a daylight/indoor light switch, also called a white balancing switch. White balancing tells the camera what "white" is—the camera adjusts for the other colors from there. Some newer cameras come with an automatic white balancing feature, which can be very convenient. If your camera is not automatic, you must place something white—a shirt, poster, or piece of paper—in the lighting you will be using and press the white balance switch. You must fill the frame with the white object—zoom in so only the white shows—and turn on all sources of light. This will fine-tune the camera.

If everything in a taped scene is off color, you probably forgot to adjust the white balance.

Don't forget to readjust the camera every time you move to different lighting!

SOUND

Student videographers usually obtain adequate sound from the microphone built into the camera. Be aware, however, that the built-in microphone will pick up sound from everywhere, including the cameraperson. Furthermore, the sound of the cameraperson may be recorded more loudly than any other sound because he or she is closer to the microphone! Also beware of fluorescent lights—they hum!

Although the built-in microphone is usually sufficient, at certain times additional microphones may be needed, such as for an interview or when recording in a large room. Sound or "audio" techniques can be complex—which is why many professionals make a living doing sound—but they need not be overwhelming. If students want to use additional microphones in their video production, ask your school's theater or music instructor for help, contact your local music store for suggestions, or check your local library for additional references.

If you want to add sound to your completed videotape or change the sound you have, you will need to undertake some "audio dubbing." This is explained further on p. 29.

GRAPHICS

Graphics is the name generally applied to the signs or written material used in a video production—the title, credits, and so forth. If you want graphics to appear in your finished videotape, you will need to create them to record on camera. Every student seems to enjoy creating graphics.

One word of caution: since you will be aiming the camera at the graphic and then recording it, the display must fill the frame completely. You do not want to record the wooden chair supporting the posterboard in your attempt to squeeze in all the credit lines! This means students must leave a border around the edge of the posterboard. Three or four inches all the way around should suffice. Encourage students to use the center of the posterboard for their graphic, remembering that a television screen is proportioned on a 4 x 3 ratio: four units across by three units down. A television screen is not square. If students keep forgetting to leave a margin, cut

a mask to fit over the posterboard and have them trace it on the board before they begin.

What materials to use? Try butcher paper, posterboard, magnetic letters on the blackboard, letters on a feltboard, flying letters (letters suspended with fishline), press-type, computer-generated graphics, and so forth. You will also need plenty of markers, glue, scissors, and erasers!

What graphics to include? You might consider preparing a title for your video production, credits, transitions (such as "two days later" or "meanwhile"), and, of course, "The End"!

See p. 81 in the appendix for further information on materials for the classroom, including how to prepare graphics and overhead transparencies. Explore all the resources (people, space, and materials) available to you in your school and community.

PRODUCTION CUES AND GESTURES

Many cues and gestures are used in video productions. Some are related to technical actions and expectations that amateur student crews need not know. Other basic gestures can simplify production work, however, and give a sense of professionalism to the production crew. Some of the basic gestures are illustrated at right. They are further explained in Lesson 3 (p. 42).

5-4-3-2-1   STAND BY   SPEED UP   READY

CUT   STRETCH   ACTION   OK

EDITING

Editing is the arranging of taped scenes or "takes" into a finished form. There are two types of editing, in-camera editing and machine-to-machine editing.

In-Camera Editing

In-camera editing simply means that you tape the scenes in the order in which they will appear in the final video. You can tape several takes of one scene, but each time you tape, you will need to rewind the tape to the beginning of the previous take, and the previous take will be erased.

If you decide to tape only one take of each scene, you simply tape your beginning graphics, then pause or stop the camera and prepare the first scene. You tape the first scene, then pause or stop the camera and prepare the second scene, then tape the second scene and so forth until the video is finished. No further editing is required.

Machine-to-Machine Editing

Machine-to-machine editing allows you to essentially reassemble the finished tape in any order you choose. This means you can tape the scenes in the order that is the easiest and put the takes together later in the proper sequence. This also means that you can save all the takes you might make of a single scene and choose the best one during editing.

Machine-to-machine editing can be done with two VCRs or, better, professional editing equipment. Portable editors are also available that do a passable edit. Your local video dealer can provide more information.

Before you start you must log your tape, that is, review it slowly and take note of each scene and the counter numbers at which each scene appears. This is discussed in detail in Lesson 8 (p. 62). A blank Edit Log form is included in the appendix on p. 88.

Once the tape is logged and you have chosen the scenes you want to appear in the finished video, you are ready to begin editing. If you are using two VCRs, machine-to-machine editing can be done in two ways, depending on the kind of VCR you have, so check your manual.

PRODUCTION TECHNIQUES

Hook-up. One VCR will be the "player" and one will be the "recorder." You will need a monitor for each. You will also need two separate cables with the correct plugs or a double Y cable with separate plugs. (These are available at your local electronics store.) One cable connects the player VCR audio "out" with the recorder VCR audio "in," and one cable connects the video "out" on the player VCR to the video "in" on the recorder VCR. See your VCR manual for more specific instructions.

Timing. An important thing to remember is that both VCRs need about 5 seconds to get their tapes rolling at proper recording speed, that is, 5 seconds of stable video signal before editing can begin. Failure to get up to speed results in "rainbows" or other distortions on the tape for the first few seconds. Both of the following procedures allow for 5 seconds of rolling time to get up speed before the taping starts.

Procedure 1.
- Insert a blank tape in the recorder VCR and your logged tape in the player VCR.
- Find the spot on the blank tape where you wish to begin (or resume) taping. Using your logging notes, find the scene on your logged tape that you wish to record.
- Set the counters at zero on both machines. Rewind both tapes about 5 counter numbers.
- Put the machines in "play," then hit the "pause" buttons when the counters are two digits from zero. Now put both machines in play again simultaneously.
- When the counters reach zero, hit the "record" button on the recorder VCR and let both machines roll until the end of the scene. Stop the machines, recue them, and begin the process again.

Procedure 2.
- Insert a blank tape in the recorder VCR and your logged tape in the player VCR.
- Find the spot on the blank tape where you wish to begin (or resume) taping. Using your logging notes, find the scene on your logged tape that you wish to record.
- Set the counters at zero on both machines.
- Put the recorder VCR into "record" and then "pause." Rewind the logged tape on the player VCR about 10 counter numbers, then hit "play."
- When the beginning of the scene appears, take the recorder VCR out of pause to begin the recording (read your manual on this procedure for specific directions, however, because machines vary).
- Let both machines roll until the end of the scene. Stop the machines, recue them, and begin the process again.

You must practice, practice, practice! The only way to become adept at smooth, clean transitions between scenes is to practice. One nice thing about machine-to-machine editing, however, is that if you make a mistake, you can simply do it over!

AUDIO DUBBING

The type of VCR you have will determine if you can add sound or change sound on your tape. Review your manual for directions. One word of advice: if you are going to play with audio dubbing, make a copy of your tape and experiment with the copy to avoid erasing the audio on your original tape!

Stereo Sound. If your VCR is a stereo VCR, you can put additional sound on one electronic track and leave the original sound on the other track (for example, to add background music to an ocean shore scene). A stereo VCR should have two audio inputs for left- and right-hand channels. If it has only one input, check with your video dealer for an adapter.

Sound-on-Sound. This feature allows you to add additional sound to the existing sound on your tape. See your VCR manual for directions.

Audio Dubbing. On some VCRs, adding additional sound to a tape means erasing the original sound. Newer VCRs have a special feature called "audio dub" that allows you to add sound without losing the original sound. See your VCR manual for directions.

VIDEO CREW

A video crew can consist of many people, but at least four positions are critical: producer, director, cameraperson, and "talent." Light and sound technicians may also be valuable, as well as a video technician. Each position has specific duties during the preproduction phase of the project, during production, and during postproduction. These duties are outlined at right.

Producer (The Boss!)

Preproduction

- makes the final decision on the content, audience, and objectives of the production
- chooses and assigns responsibility to the director and lets the director choose, but has final say over, the scriptwriter(s), storyboard artist(s), crew members, and talent

Production

- oversees production but is not involved in the day-to-day responsibility unless he or she desires or is asked

Postproduction

- participates in logging and editing the tapes
- evaluates the artistic and technical quality of the production

Director

Preproduction

- is responsible for preparing the script and storyboard (although he or she may assign someone else to complete them)
- is responsible for the preparation of prop and equipment lists and the diagram of the set
- trains crew members for their various jobs
- calls for walk-throughs and rehearsals

Production

- calls the camera shots
- cues the talent and crew
- interprets the script and storyboard for the talent and crew

Postproduction

- participates in logging and editing the tapes
- evaluates the artistic and technical quality of the production

Cameraperson

Preproduction
- makes sure the crew members know their duties
- makes sure the crew members do their jobs
- helps prepare the set and props
- is familiar with the script and storyboard

Production
- operates the camera following the director's commands

Postproduction
- helps the director evaluate the production
- supervises the crew in disconnecting equipment and putting everything away

Talent

Preproduction
- helps crew members as needed
- memorizes the script and storyboard
- is ready for walk-throughs and rehearsals

Production
- follows the director's cues
- thinks about his or her part and characterization

Postproduction
- helps evaluate the production
- helps put away the equipment

Light and Sound Technicians

Preproduction
- arrange for lighting and sound following the director's wishes

Production
- provide adequate light and sound during taping following director and cameraperson's commands
- help set up and put away equipment

Video Technician

Production
- runs VCR if separate from camera
- provides appropriate cues (such as "tape rolling")
- helps set up and put away equipment

Other crew positions may be necessary depending on the size of the production. These include a prop or set person, a costumes and makeup person, and a graphics person. Positions can be created as needed!

HINTS AND CAUTIONS

To prevent permanent damage to the camera, always point the camera away from the sun or lights. When the camera is not in use, keep the lens cap on. (This is the responsibility of the cameraperson.)

Check all your cable connections. Tape a trial scene and review it. One class lost a whole day's taping because the microphone cord was not properly attached and no sound was recorded. (One way to avoid this particular mishap is to use headphones and monitor what is being recorded.)

Check all your equipment for tight attachments. You would hate to lose a camera because of a loose screw or bolt.

Make all camera moves S-L-O-W-L-Y. Pan, tilt, and zoom carefully.

Special effects can get boring quickly. Do not overdo them.

Remember to white balance before you begin and every time the lighting changes.

Label all tapes (date, subject, approximate length of recording).

Do not leave the camera in "pause" for too long. It will wear out your tape and dirty the heads of your VCR. If you will not be recording for a while, turn the camera to "stop."

Vary shots to add interest. Try taping each scene from different angles.

If you want to save your tape, break out the "erase-protect" tab (see the instructions that come with the tape).

VIDEO PRODUCTION IN 9 EASY LESSONS

Lesson 1 **What Makes an Effective Production?**

Lesson 2 **The Mechanics: Simple Scripts and Storyboards**

Lesson 3 **Introducing Equipment: Producing a Simple Interview**

Lesson 4 **Selecting a Program Treatment**

Lesson 5 **Production: Technique, Terminology, Technicians**

Lesson 6 **Finalizing the Video Production Proposal**

Lesson 7 **The Production!**

Lesson 8 **Logging and Editing Rough Footage**

Lesson 9 **Evaluation, Student-style**

LESSON 1
WHAT MAKES AN EFFECTIVE PRODUCTION?

TEACHER'S OBJECTIVES

- to review the elements of any production—theme, setting, plot, mood, characterizations.
- to help students analyze a production for its elements.
- to help students understand the importance of the relationships among production elements.
- to help students construct a chart of criteria to use in evaluating productions.

STUDENTS' OBJECTIVES

- to identify the elements of a video production.
- to identify the effective qualities of a television show.
- to analyze and evaluate a current high-quality television show.

FUNDAMENTALS

Before students can begin to produce videos, they need to evaluate the qualities of *effective* video productions. Just about all students have seen effective video productions, but usually they have not analyzed them for the elements that make them effective. Students will need to pay attention to these elements to use them effectively.

One concept that is crucial to video production is "layering." Layering is present in every effective production. It is the deliberate choice of elements that appeal to a variety of audiences. For example, *All in the Family*, a popular situation comedy from the 1970s, appealed to a variety of people because

- the characters represented several age groups,
- politics and racism, even feminism, were brought up in the series and each attracted its share of the audience,
- the interactions of the characters were readily identifiable to a majority of the audience (we all argued these issues at home, too!),

- the characterizations, although stereotypical, were generic enough that each audience member could identify with a character's good points and bad ones (we were drawn to these contradictions—we found them humorous), and
- the plots were realistic in the way problems arose and delightful in the creative and comic way in which problems were solved.

Nevertheless, simply throwing together a variety of elements (such as certain distinct personalities) without thinking about their "fit" to the characters, theme, setting, plot, or mood does not guarantee success. The point is: *It is the conscious use of related elements that appeal to various audiences at the same time that makes a video effective.* It is the interplay among these elements that makes the magic work. All successful programs have layering.

STUDENTS WILL NEED TO KNOW

- theme, setting, plot, mood, and characterization as elements of any production.
- how to be able to analyze a production for these elements.
- popular television shows either past or present.

MATERIALS

- a preselected written work to analyze in class. Suggestions include a selection from Junior Great Books, Mother Goose poems, or a fable or myth such as Snow White.
- a preselected video recording of a current high-quality television show to analyze in class.
- a chalkboard and chalk or chart paper and markers.
- a VCR (video cassette recorder) and television to show the video recording cited above.

VOCABULARY*

Characterizations

Criteria

Mood

Plot

Setting

Theme

* Vocabulary words are defined in the glossary, p. 91.

PROCEDURES

Preparation: Ask students if they have ever created their own television show and ask if it was a lot of work. Tell them that television can be a lot of fun if they understand the basics of producing shows. Tell them that by the end of the day's lesson they will understand what makes a good television show great.

1. BRAINSTORM TV SHOWS. Ask students to think of the names of television shows past and present. Record all answers on the chalkboard. Then have students name past and present "hit" shows, ones that were successful or popular according to students. Add these to the list on the board. Guide this compilation so that it includes "classic" shows (those generally recognized for high quality), especially those currently in syndication.

2. COMPARE MOST AND LEAST FAVORITE SHOWS. Ask students to name their favorite shows and record these answers on the chalkboard for comparison. Then ask students to name their least favorite programs and list these names as well. Compare these two lists and discuss, using the following questions to begin the discussion:

Are any shows on both lists?
Why did you choose each particular show?
How have your choices changed as you have grown older?
What could account for the differences in choices?

3. RECALL THE ELEMENTS OF A DRAMATIC WORK. Ask students to identify the elements of a book. They are theme, setting, plot, characterization, and mood. Have students define the elements and give examples of each. Select a television show from the previous lists and analyze it for its elements.

4. ANALYZE A WORK FOR ITS ELEMENTS. Have students analyze your preselected written work for its elements.

5. ANALYZE THE ELEMENTS FOR EFFECTIVENESS. Ask students, "What makes a *good* plot?" Then, "What makes a *good* theme?" You will probably get answers like "those that are realistic, believable, original." Have students discuss the characteristics of effective elements. This will lead them to discover interrelationships among elements. Someone will probably say, "The setting must match the theme . . . ." Point out that to be effective, the elements must "fit" with each other in this way. Ask students to provide other examples.

6. CONSTRUCT A "CRITERIA FOR EVALUATION" CHART. Have students synthesize the discussion by constructing a Criteria for Evaluation chart. This chart will include observations and requirements noted by the students, for example, "Does the setting match the theme in time?" Point out that, to be effective, the chart must be applicable to any video production with a script. (News, educational television, and documentaries are excluded!) Post this chart in a conspicuous location and use it frequently!

7. EVALUATE A FAVORITE TV SHOW USING THIS CHART. Discuss the "hit" shows listed on the board for a few minutes by asking the students, "Why are these shows successful?" This serves to refresh students' memories about the shows and also to familiarize everyone with the basic concepts of the shows cited.

8. EVALUATE A PRESELECTED TV SHOW USING THIS CHART. Let's hope that your prerecorded tape will be of a television show on the students' list. Have the class watch a selection from the show, perhaps even an entire program, and then analyze the show for its elements using the Criteria for Evaluation chart.

9. HOMEWORK ACTIVITY. Students should choose a popular dramatic television program (not a game show or a documentary) and analyze it for the basic story elements discussed thus far. This should be a written review.

EXTENSION ACTIVITY

Students could create an outline of the basic story elements for an original dramatic television script. The outline should include a description of the main characters, a description of the setting, a summary of the plot, a description of the mood, and a statement of the theme.

LESSON 2
THE MECHANICS: SIMPLE SCRIPTS AND STORYBOARDS

TEACHER'S OBJECTIVES

- to define the specialized terminology appropriate to video scripts and storyboards.
- to help each student create a script and storyboard for a simple interview.

STUDENTS' OBJECTIVES

- to identify basic production terminology and techniques.
- to develop a simple script.
- to develop a simple storyboard.
- to use a variety of camera angles and shots in creating a script and storyboard.

FUNDAMENTALS

Having analyzed the elements that contribute to effective video productions, students can now better understand production elements—what converts ideas into reality. A script and a storyboard help structure ideas into practical, cohesive concepts that have form and flow.

STUDENTS WILL NEED TO KNOW

- the meaning of the terms "audio" and "video."

MATERIALS

- overhead transparencies* of the sample script and storyboard sheets (pp. 82-84) and markers.
- blank copies of the script and storyboard forms as worksheets (pp. 86-87).
- optional: transparencies of video equipment, camera shots, and camera transitions (see **The Basics** and **Production Techniques**)
- a demonstration set-up: camera, lights (if necessary), and, if possible, a monitor connected to the camera so students can see what the cameraperson sees.

VOCABULARY

Close-up

Cut

Fade in/fade out

Long shot

Medium shot

Pan

Tilt

Zoom in/zoom out

* See "Materials for the Classroom" (p. 81) in the appendix for information on how to prepare transparencies and other materials for classroom demonstration.

PROCEDURES

Preparation: Ask students if any of them has ever been on television or visited a television studio. Share their experiences for a moment, then tell students that by the end of the day's lesson, they will have planned their own short interview in which each class member will get to be on camera. (Ignore the groans now—they will really enjoy this!)

1. IDENTIFY VIDEO EQUIPMENT.
Ask students to list types of equipment used in a television studio. You might want to display overhead transparencies of "Basic Equipment" (pp. 9-15) to fill in any gaps in their knowledge. Relate their list to the equipment you plan to use in your classroom. For example, if you will not be using separate microphones, point this out.

2. IDENTIFY CAMERA SHOTS.
Next, use the camera and a transparency of "The Camera—Shots" (p.16) and point out differences among shots. The dem-

onstration is important: it is good practice for you and it increases your credibility with students. If some students are proficient with a camera, have them demonstrate some shots. If they have not yet used a video camera, go easy on the demonstrations until later.

For practice, have students identify the various camera shots used in a specific short video sequence such as a commercial, an introduction to a television show, or a news commentary.

3. IDENTIFY CAMERA TRANSITIONS.
Display a transparency of "The Camera—Movement" (p. 19) and "The Camera—Transitions" (p. 20) and discuss transitions. Demonstrate each transition, being sure that students know what knobs, buttons, or levers produce each effect when using your equipment. Remember, you are not only teaching terminology, you are also familiarizing students with the equipment so they can make a video production. Have students demonstrate each of these moves.

4. IDENTIFY PARTS OF A SCRIPT.
Tell students that today they will be creating their own scripts and storyboards for a real video. Display a transparency (or distribute copies) of the sample script (p. 83). Ask students to note that the script is divided into two sections—"Audio" and "Video."

5. DEFINE THE PURPOSES OF THE AUDIO AND VIDEO SECTIONS OF A SCRIPT.
Using the sample script, have students note that the audio section of the script details the spoken or audio section of the production. Words to be spoken are written in capital and lower-case letters. The video portion contains directions for the cameraperson, director, and other crewmembers. These directions are always written in capital letters. Point out the terminology used and indicate that, in creating a script, the writer must anticipate the visual shot needed for each section.

6. IDENTIFY PARTS OF A STORYBOARD. Display a transparency (or distribute copies) of the sample storyboard (p.84) from the same sample production as the script. Ask students to differentiate between the script and the storyboard. Note that the purpose of a storyboard is not to be artistic but to give a visual impression of each scene. Also note that camera transitions are identified between the scenes of the storyboard to clarify how the cameraperson moves from one shot to another. As practice, you might want to create a simple storyboard together in class, using an overhead transparency storyboard form.

7. CREATE A SIMPLE SCRIPT. Divide the class into groups of three or four students (or let the students choose their own groups). These groups will be working together for a while, so be sure they can work together! Now direct each group to create its own short interview with the following structure: a host or hostess greets the television audience, introduces the guest and identifies the guest's purpose for appearing, asks the guest one simple question that the guest answers, then thanks the guest for appearing and the television audience for watching. Each group should use a blank script sheet (p. 86). The students may be as creative as they can in naming the show, the host or hostess, and the guest and in writing the conversation. (Students can also be creative with the camerawork, but for the moment, encourage them to contain their creativity to the audio portion of the script.)

Have the groups write out their planned interview, taking care to draw lines between any sections of dialogue that are separated by camera cuts. Remind them of the use of capital and lower-case letters for the audio section of the script and capitals only for the video section.

8. CREATE A SIMPLE STORYBOARD. As soon as each group agrees on the basics of its script, start some members of each group on their storyboard. The storyboard should illustrate the script that each group is writing.

Remember: each group is writing only one script and storyboard. In the next lesson, each member of the group will rotate in the jobs of host or hostess, guest, cameraperson, and director for his or her group's script.

You may want to collect the groups' scripts and storyboards and make copies for each member, or they can make their own. When each group has completed its script and storyboard, members may spend extra time "blocking" their script, that is, rehearsing the script as if they were actually recording it. They could even create backdrops or costumes. This is fine and fun, but do not let the embellishments take away from the real purpose: constructing effective scripts and storyboards.

Remind the groups that each member will get to act each part and will be taped doing it!

Next comes the FUN PART!

LESSON 3
INTRODUCING EQUIPMENT: PRODUCING A SIMPLE INTERVIEW

TEACHER'S OBJECTIVES

- to assist students in the production of a short video interview.
- to encourage students to use a variety of camera angles and shots in their camerawork.
- to demonstrate the use of correct directing terminology and gestures.
- to demonstrate correct framing techniques.

STUDENTS' OBJECTIVES

- to define the roles of the video production personnel.
- to effectively use a script, storyboard, and production techniques to complete a video interview.
- to use a video camera competently.
- to use simple directing techniques effectively.

FUNDAMENTALS

Students will apply what they have learned in the two previous lessons to produce an effective interview. The main purpose of this lesson is to familiarize students with the video camera—being both in front of and behind it—and to use correct directing techniques.

THE TEACHER WILL NEED TO KNOW

- how to use the camera to achieve a close-up, medium shot, long shot, fade in, fade out, zoom in, zoom out, cut, pan, and tilt.
- basic lighting. A simple lighting set-up will suffice (see "Lighting," p. 23).
- how to record with the camera and play back the tape on a monitor using the camcorder or a VCR.

- simple camera framing techniques (see "The Camera—Framing the Shot," p. 18).
- the duties of the director, the cameraperson, and talent (see "Video Crew," p. 30). It is especially important to stress the hierarchy of responsibility within the video crew. If you strictly enforce that the sole job of the cameraperson is to operate the camera under the direction of the director, and something goes wrong, then the culprit will be obvious. Remember, the director is *headquarters*. He or she tells everyone what to do, and if the talent or the cameraperson does not like it—well, that person can be director *next* time!

STUDENTS WILL NEED TO KNOW

- how to read a script and story-board.
- how to use the camera in a simple fashion.

MATERIALS

- a set-up for taping the interviews (a camera with a VCR or camcorder, tripod, and so forth; see pp. 9-15).
- simple lighting (see p. 23).
- simple background: a desk and two chairs for the interview is fine!
- videotapes—one should do!
- a monitor: having a monitor rigged to a VCR (if you are using a separate camera and VCR) or to the camcorder is exceedingly helpful. Not only can the director see what the cameraperson sees, but the entire class will watch avidly so that they can do better when it's their turn!
- yarn and masking tape.
- sample photographs: you may want to have posters or pictures of famous photographs for the students to analyze when discussing composition.

VOCABULARY

"Cut"

Ready cue

"Roll tape"

"Stand by"

"Tape rolling"

Time cues ("5,4,3,2,1")

"You're on" (action)

PROCEDURES

Preparation: Remind students that each person will get the chance to be the host or hostess, guest, cameraperson, and director. Each team will rotate jobs until every member has had a turn in each job. At the end of the lesson, all teams will view the tape and critique each video for both good and bad points. Also, tell students that they will be learning a simple "trick" to make their video and even their photographs more interesting!

If a team has only three members, you can rotate into the fourth position or ask for a student volunteer. Having the teacher on the crew can provide a more adult example of proper behavior and technique.

Be sure to be lavish in your praise of good points and keep any negative comments brief, infrequent, and constructive. Encourage students to do the same. See p. 80 for some positive comments you can use.

1. LOCATE EFFECTIVE FRAMING POINTS.

Basic camera shot composition is important. Using the camera and monitor, have a "victim" sit on the set and divide the screen into thirds horizontally and vertically by taping yarn across the monitor.

Tell the class that the basic idea is to place the main element(s) on the screen at one of the four intersections where the yarn crosses. Also point out that the eyes of a person on the screen are usually placed on an imaginary line two-thirds of the way up from the bottom of the screen. Demonstrate this using the camera and monitor.

This is a good time to display some famous photographs and to analyze composition. If none are available, ask students to bring in examples of well-composed photographs and to watch for effective composition as they watch television.

2. DEFINE THE ROLES OF DIRECTOR, CAMERAPERSON, AND TALENT.

Discuss with the class the various roles they will be undertaking. Point out that the job of the "talent" (the host or hostess and guest) is to interpret his or her role but only with the approval of the director. The cameraperson also does only what the director says. If the director forgets to say "cut!" then the cameraperson does not cut. It is much easier later on if these roles are clear from the beginning. Remind students: *This is not a democratic project!*

3. DEMONSTRATE EFFECTIVE DIRECTING TECHNIQUES.

Walk the students through a sample interview with you as director. The sequence should go as follows:

- Once the talent is in place and the cameraperson is ready, the director shouts, "Stand by!" This is done only to inform the people nearby that taping is imminent. Upon hearing this, all audible talking and noise should stop. Do not let students use this at other times to get quiet!
- The director, holding his or her hand in a "ready" cue, looks around the room to determine the readiness of the group. The

director then turns to the cameraperson and says, "Roll tape."

- The cameraperson starts recording and checks to see that the tape is rolling by watching the VCR counters or light in the camera monitor. (This can be done by another person at the VCR if the VCR is separate.) The cameraperson (or person at the VCR) responds, "Tape rolling." Be sure the tape *is* rolling!

- The director places a hand where the talent will be looking when the scene begins (for example, next to the camera lens if the talent is looking directly at the camera) and gestures 5, 4, 3, 2, 1 while simultaneously calling "5, 4, 3 . . . ." The director does not call "2, 1." Allowing five seconds of "roll time" at the beginning and end of each scene is necessary for editing later on. NEVER SKIP THIS STEP!

- When the director points at or cues the talent, the talent begins the scene and continues until the end of the scene. At the end of

the scene, the talent freezes and the director gestures 5, 4, 3, 2, 1 while simultaneously calling " . . . 3, 2, 1, CUT!" Note that the director does not call "5, 4 . . . " NEVER SKIP THIS STEP! Do not allow students to play around with these steps. You will see how drastically important they are when you edit, believe me.

4. VIDEOTAPE. Now we're ready! Select a group to begin and instruct the other groups to watch. You may want to act as director the first time. Have students select their roles. Quickly review with the cameraperson the various switches and buttons that he or she will need to know. While the cameraperson experiments with the camera, instruct the talent to review their script. If you are not the director, review the director's steps with the person in that role.

Make sure everything is ready (lights? sound? VCR? tape?) and GO!

After the first round with this brave group, stop, rewind the tape,

and view it. Check for sound levels, lighting, and so forth. The group will die of embarrassment. Smile! Now rotate places and repeat.

Tape all the groups so that every student has a chance at every role. Do not allow anyone to back out of a part. Tell them they must do this simple experiment now to understand what they will do later. Tell them they can choose the role they would like in subsequent lessons. For now, they need to try all the roles.

5. EVALUATE. At the end of the session, view the tape from the entire session. Do not take the yarn off the monitor. Let students see for themselves that what they see in the camera viewfinder is not necessarily what comes on the screen. Again, be lavish in your positive feedback and easy on the criticism. Students will be self-critical enough without your help. Remind them that this is only the beginning and the object of this lesson was to learn to use the video equipment. Tell them you did not expect perfection (this time). Smile!

LESSON 4
SELECTING A PROGRAM TREATMENT

TEACHER'S OBJECTIVES

- to help students select a video treatment for their original production.
- to help students generate ideas for their video production.

STUDENTS' OBJECTIVES

- to differentiate among types of program treatments.
- to select a program treatment for the video production.
- to participate in the initial planning for a video production.

FUNDAMENTALS

Now students can begin work on their own video productions. Allow students to work as a class or in small, self-selected groups. This usually requires a class discussion, and the class may not be ready to choose at this time. (Some students may want to see what the whole group is doing before they decide to do their own production. This is fine to a point, but make a deadline after which students cannot switch.)

Soon students will begin to meet in their production teams to discuss choices and arrange duties. The first big decision each team should reach is what kind of video to do.

Regarding the size of each team, only you know your class well enough to structure this requirement. I have found that when my entire class has worked on a single project, things have been much simpler, but I have also had excellent results with smaller groups within a class. For your sanity, try to limit the number of groups within a classroom to four.

THE TEACHER WILL NEED TO KNOW

- the differences among the various types of program treatments: documentary, humorous, dramatic, educational, or combinations of these (see "Choice of Video Treatment," p. 22).
- the steps each production team must go through to produce a finished video. The students will be developing a Video Production Proposal that will structure their thoughts and enthusiasm, but you will need to focus their energies in specific directions at certain times. At this point the primary focus should be on the completion of the Video Production Proposal. Once students complete each section of the proposal, the team will have a more specific direction for their production.

Keep in mind at this early stage that students must choose the kind of editing they will do *before they begin:*

1. In-camera editing, which requires that students record each scene (and graphic) in the order in which it will appear, or

2. Machine-to-machine editing, which allows students to record several takes of each scene in non-sequential order and later reassemble the tape into finished form.

In-camera editing requires careful planning and coordination during recording but no further editing after the taping is finished. You have your finished product! Machine-to-machine editing gives you greater flexibility during recording, but it requires a lot of editing time later.

STUDENTS WILL NEED TO KNOW

- camera shots and transitions discussed in the last lesson.
- the basic purpose of a script and storyboard.

MATERIALS

- copies of the Video Production Proposal (pp. 78-79).
- optional: videotapes of previous student productions.
- optional: a transparency of "Choice of Video Treatment" (p. 22).

VOCABULARY

Types of treatments:

Dramatic

Documentary

Educational

Humorous

PROCEDURES

Preparation: Tell students that this is the day on which they will begin planning their own original video production. If you have a special goal for this video (for example, to show it at an open house or to enter it in a contest), explain it at this time. Give the class a rough sense of the schedule (for example, "We have three weeks in which to plan, tape, and complete this video. Planning will take at least one week . . ."). Tell students that they can decide how to work on this video— whether in teams or as an entire class—but first you need to describe the kinds of videos they can produce.

1. DIFFERENTIATE AMONG TYPES OF PROGRAM TREATMENTS. You may want to display a transparency of "Choice of Video Treatment." Review and discuss the various types of program treatments such as educational, dramatic, humorous, and documentary. Ask students to provide examples of each of these and to think of examples of programs that combine treatments. Point out that a video project does not have to be dramatic or have a storyline. One class I taught did a wonderful job of videotaping interviews with kindergarten students to show to incoming kindergartners, along with a companion video interviewing school personnel to show to the parents of the incoming students. Point out that often videos take an "old" subject or storyline and give it a new "twist"—a new theme, characters, mood, or setting.

2. BEGIN PLANNING THE VIDEO PRODUCTION. Have students discuss how they would like to group themselves for this project. The discussion may take some time, or the class may be quite singleminded. Try to hear all points of view. Guide the discussion if necessary to avoid personal comments. This discussion should reflect the goals and desires of students. After twenty minutes, end the discussion by pointing out that the final decision does not have to be reached yet. Tell students they can use some time to mull over their ideas. Announce that the final decision must be reached by the time production proposals are submitted, however, and give that date.

Now brainstorm with the class about the embryonic ideas they may have for videos. Place all these ideas on the blackboard and keep them there until the next class. Do not discuss any idea in detail. Praise students' participation. In your discussion, try to combine ideas or give them new twists. (In one of my classes, my students, who knew I was a member of an acting company that staged "murder weekends," were tickled when I suggested combining their idea of a kiddie video on dolls with a murder mystery. This developed into a wonderful murder mystery in which the dolls made their owners disappear.) Keep your comments light, supportive, and positive.

3. STRUCTURE THE PRODUCTION PROCESS. Drawing an analogy to an iceberg, point out to the class that planning takes the most amount of time in any good production. Although the final production may last fifteen minutes, many hours will be, and must be, spent in planning. This is the purpose of the Video Production Proposal: it forces students to plan. *Planning,* during which students will decide on their video's purpose, audience, elements, point of view, and format, will lead directly to *design,* during which students will develop script, storyboard, budget, and special needs such as props or costumes. Once the design

is completed, *production* can begin. After production, *evaluation* is necessary to complete the process.

4. INTRODUCE THE VIDEO PRODUCTION PROPOSAL. Distribute copies of the Video Production Proposal form and go over each step. Tell students that before design can begin, the Video Production Proposal must be approved by the executive producer—you!

Sometimes students get obsessed with violence and simple solutions to problems in their scripts. Invariably, videos in this format end up being superficial and boring. Be firm with these students in your demand for more thought and depth in their scripts. This is a good time to share videos from previous classes or other groups of students and analyze them based on the criteria developed by the class in Lesson 1 on effective videos. I have tried letting students produce superficial videos (although I toned down the violence) and I found that letting them "fall on their faces" is not

educationally effective here. They did not learn to change their scripts. It is effective to show these superficial videos to other classes, however, for evaluation. Students readily see the lack of quality. Include in the discussion reviews or critical comments from previous years as well, if you have them.

Now let students go and work on their Video Production Proposals!

LESSON 5
PRODUCTION: TECHNIQUE, TERMINOLOGY, TECHNICIANS

TEACHER'S OBJECTIVES

- to help students complete a script and storyboard for their video project.
- to define the roles of the members of the production crew.

STUDENTS' OBJECTIVES

- to define the basic roles of the production crewmembers.
- to choose a format, purpose, audience, materials, and budget for their video project as outlined on the Video Production Proposal.
- to participate effectively on a planning team for a video production.

FUNDAMENTALS

You have started students in the production of their first video. Congratulations! Things may seem embryonic right now, but that is all right! You are at the mess stage in creative production. Soon vague hunches will begin to solidify into workable ideas. Be patient!

In this lesson students will select a format for their video, complete their production proposal, begin writing their script and storyboard, decide on crewmembers, and assign duties. They will make great strides toward the final realization of their production.

All this time students will be making major decisions about what they want to do for their video. These decisions are still flexible and may change as teams revise their perception of what they can and cannot practically do. The makeup of the crews can remain flexible right through the taping with the exception of the producer and director. The producer—remember, you are the executive producer!—is the final authority. He or she retains the right to "fire" or "hire" the director and crewmembers. Encourage your producer to keep these power plays at a minimum.

The director is charged with getting the concept of the video on tape. He or she makes the script come to life, with real talent and real scenery. Because it is reality, however, the director's concept and the producer's concept may not match. It is the teacher's job to make sure that the producers and directors understand this fact and deal with it constructively.

THE TEACHER WILL NEED TO KNOW

- the responsibilities of each crew-member and the pecking order (see "Video Crew," p. 30).
- how to produce effective graphics (see "Graphics," p. 25).

STUDENTS WILL NEED TO KNOW

- how to create a script and storyboard.
- how to develop a Video Production Proposal.

MATERIALS

- copies of "Video Crew."

VOCABULARY

Audience

Director

Point of view

Producer

Talent

Teamwork

PROCEDURES

Preparation: Ask the class how they have decided to work. All groups should be solidified enough so that today they can choose their crewmembers and begin working in earnest. If a group is not this far, you may need to step in as executive producer and make some decisions for them. By the end of today's class, each group will have a producer and possibly a director. The main goal for this class is to complete the Video Production Proposal.

1. DEFINE THE BASIC ROLES OF THE VIDEO CREW. Distribute copies of "Video Crew." Review the duties of each technician and make sure that students understand not only what each technician does, but who has responsibility for what. Inform the class that you will support the following chain of command: if the cameraperson has a problem, he or she should go to the director first, then to the producer, and only then to the executive producer (you). The students will test this structure in the beginning, but if you stick to your word, they will learn to work out their differences among themselves, as they should.

2. CHOOSE A PRODUCER. Ask each group to choose a producer and notify you of their choice. This person will answer to you. Make sure the group and the producer understand their responsibilities.

Can the producer be in the video? Yes, although I have discouraged it. I have found it works better if the producer stays detached. There are plenty of other jobs—graphics, costumes, props, even directing—that he or she can do during production. Can the director be in the video? Again, say no initially, but if during production you discover you need the director in the video, do it.

Other crewmembers can be in the video when they are not needed for their job. Producers, directors, and others can be in another group's video if desired, but another group's video cannot conflict with their video. The home team comes first!

3. CHOOSE A DIRECTOR. Have each group's producer choose a director. This is the group's first experience with the hierarchy. If you have convinced them of the need for a definite structure, you will have no problems here. Allow groups to have two directors if they are large (ten or more members).

4. FINISH THE VIDEO PRODUCTION PROPOSAL. If a group has not done so, it should now be working together under its producer and director to complete its Video Production Proposal, write a script, and create storyboards. Lots of work here! Make sure producers keep every member of their team busy.

5. ASSIGN THE REST OF THE VIDEO CREW. Once you have accepted and approved a group's Video Production Proposal, the director can begin to assign crew duties. A group may want to hold auditions. (The director decides! The producer can override the director, but discourage this.) In the next lesson, groups will choose lighting, sound, and graphics for their videos. This is becoming a reality!

LESSON 6
FINALIZING THE VIDEO PRODUCTION PROPOSAL

TEACHER'S OBJECTIVES

- to assist students in the final preparations for their video productions.
- to outline procedures and techniques in creating graphics.
- to demonstrate correct and effective techniques for lighting and sound.
- to assist in final rehearsals and run-throughs.

STUDENTS' OBJECTIVES

- to complete the initial planning and the Video Production Proposal.
- to create effective graphics if necessary for the production.
- to use sound and lighting correctly.
- to participate effectively in the group's production.

FUNDAMENTALS

Students should now be working enthusiastically on their productions. Your role will be to direct traffic. Encourage producers and directors to be responsible for the involvement of each member of their crew. You will be meeting with lighting and sound technicians to show them basic techniques.

THE TEACHER WILL NEED TO KNOW

Creating graphics for a video production can be quite simple. The important thing to remember is to leave plenty of space around the edges so the camera does not record anything beyond the edges. When my students use poster board or butcher paper, I have them leave at least three inches around the edges, and often that is too little. Investigate other options for introducing graphics in a video: use magnetic letters on a board, use a felt board, tape letters to a wall (brick is a neat texture), or use cutout letters lit from behind (see "Graphics," p. 25). Have fun with it!

Sound and lighting also need not be overwhelming, particularly if the production is simple. I have always found at least one student who preferred to do lights or sound over anything else. Often this student could handle lights and sound for every video production with a few willing assistants. (Don't be surprised if this person is a girl!)

For simple lighting, you can buy inexpensive "scoop" lights, a metal cone and a clip. These cast a harsh glare, but they are fine for beginning video productions. Be sure to use heavy-duty extension cords! (See "Lighting," p. 23, and "Sound," p. 24, for more information.)

Remember: Always point the camera away from the sun or lights! Direct light will damage the lens.

STUDENTS WILL NEED TO KNOW

By now students should have completed their scripts and storyboards and understand basic camera terminology. They should understand how to use paints, paper, glue, or whatever else they will use for their graphics.

The sound and light people should have a basic understanding of electricity, the use of wires, connections, recordings, and so forth. Remember, you do not need experts yet. This is a learning experience!

MATERIALS

- lights (at least two scoop lights).
- white posterboard for "bouncing" light on the set.
- necessary sound equipment (microphones, appropriate jacks, cords).
- materials for graphics.
- optional: transparencies of lettering styles.

VOCABULARY

Back light

Bouncing light

Graphics

Fill light

Key light

PROCEDURES

Preparation: Students will require little preparation now. Most of them will be so excited you will need to hold them back to ensure a better production. Keep their attention on details and insist that no job be rushed. Circulate among the groups and make sure everyone has something to do.

1. COMPLETE THE VIDEO PRODUCTION PROPOSAL. The main purpose of this lesson is for groups to complete their Video Production Proposals. Make sure at least part of each group is at work, revising its proposal.

2. DEFINE THE MASKING AREA FOR GRAPHICS. Help students begin their graphics. If possible, use the camera to show that the image area on the screen is not square. Standard monitors are four units across and three units down. Point out that if students extend their writing or drawing to the edges of the background, the edges of the background and beyond will show on the screen. To guard against this, they should "mask" an area at least three inches wide all the way around the background border. The more centered the graphic, the better.

3. RECOGNIZE CONTRAST PROBLEMS. Inform students that too much contrast in their graphics can actually damage the camera. Avoid using black with white, for example, or any other strongly contrasting colors.

4. IDENTIFY GRAPHICS OPTIONS. Discuss with students the variety of options available for graphics. They can use a variety of letters, background materials, or lighting. Aluminum foil can make an interesting graphic (watch lighting, though), as well as burlap or backlit lettering. Try cutting graphics out of posterboard and using fishline to "fly" them in front of the camera or use press-type, computer-generated graphics, or other commercially available lettering. Pan across the graphic or tilt the poster up or down. Be creative!

Remind the groups to anticipate and list every graphic, including ones such as "The next day . . . " or "Meanwhile. . . ."

I use a book of lettering styles to create transparencies of different lettering types. Students can trace the style they choose onto paper, cardboard, or the chalkboard. They can vary sizes and styles easily. Try it!

5. ANTICIPATE SOUND AND LIGHTING NEEDS. At this time you should have all groups of students working happily on some aspect of a video production (costumes, makeup, graphics, scripts, props, rehearsals). You will need to meet with the lighting people to explain the rudiments of lighting. You may also need to meet with the sound people if you have special audio needs in a particular video.

Have the lighting and sound people set up a few test situations and tape them, then let the technicians evaluate their tape with the director or producer. Which is most effective? Have the lighting and sound people go on location and look for potential problems. The big courtroom scene of one of my classes was almost wrecked

because the church we were using took down the drapes to clean on the day we came to tape, and huge beams of sunlight created havoc with our camera. What will the natural lighting and sound be like at the day and time you plan to tape? Will the school bus pull up during the exciting conclusion? Will the lunch bell ring just as the interview begins? Will the audience see the cameraperson's shadow? *You cannot overplan!* But remember that the video process itself often suggests solutions—it is wonderfully adaptable!

This lesson is the heart of the production. Keep everyone involved and you will find this and the next lesson the most rewarding sessions.

LESSON 7
THE PRODUCTION!

TEACHER'S OBJECTIVES

- to help groups tape a video production.
- to provide feedback as requested or necessary to maintain or improve the quality of students' productions.
- to continue to guide groups toward the completion of their productions.

STUDENTS' OBJECTIVES

- to participate constructively in the taping of a video production.

FUNDAMENTALS

Most students feel that this session is the climax of everything that has gone before. Help them keep their perspective by reminding them that this lesson is only part of the iceberg—a small part of a much larger whole. If their planning has been productive, then this session will be productive.

You may find you feel left out of this session. If your class is really hard at work and working well together, congratulations! They have been taught very well. But not every class has the maturity or ambience to work well together, so you can still play a positive role by continuing to guide the groups in their work.

Continue to keep your objectivity in case students lose theirs.

Remember, scenes may need to be shot out of sequence to best use your facilities and equipment. In addition, different groups may need to share equipment and locations. Have the directors and crews work to achieve the most efficient use of the equipment in the time you have.

It is helpful to enlist the aid of another teacher or parent to keep an eye on students not directly involved at this point. Plan to have some activities ready or ask students to bring materials to keep themselves occupied. A lot of time in production is spent simply waiting. Be prepared.

THE TEACHER WILL NEED TO KNOW

One group of students estimated that it took them seven hours of recording to get seven minutes of final tape. It always takes longer than you think! *You will always want more time! Plan for this!* My students have never finished within their schedule. We always wanted to do more or do over what we had already done.

Know when to stop. You must stop sometime. Plan on it. And let the students know.

STUDENTS WILL NEED TO KNOW

Students should be ready for just about anything. You've done a fine job! Some groups may have special needs, however. Work with them to find solutions to their problems. Although this is not network television, challenge them to find creative ways to get the effects they want!

MATERIALS

Each group should have a blank videotape for recording their production. Students will also need whatever props, materials, costumes, and so forth they anticipated in their Video Production Proposals. Expect that someone will forget something. It happens. Become a creative problem-solver.

PROCEDURES

Preparation: Make sure all equipment is collected and ready and have all materials on location. Bring extra extension cords and light bulbs!

If you are planning to edit, break down the scenes and arrange them so that all scenes at one location are shot at the same time. If you are taping your video in sequence, of course you cannot do this. If other groups plan to use a location, have them ready so they can begin to tape at that location as soon as the first group is done.

Do not allow groups to view what they have taped at this point unless another group is using the recording equipment.

Make sure your video recorder is recording at the fastest speed! High-quality editing equipment can edit only material recorded at the fastest speed. Besides, the fastest speed records the best-quality video and audio.

If you can borrow compatible equipment to use, do it! Have more than one camera at a time! But be sure the equipment is compatible.

1. TAPE THE PRODUCTIONS. Make sure everyone is involved as much as possible. Here is where producers and directors can shine. Support them in their endeavors. Roll the tape! Be sure students are following the correct procedures, especially the countdown discussed in Lesson 3. Let each tape run for one minute before you start recording. At the beginning of each take, have the sound person or the director say, "Scene ___, take ___" just after the countdown and just before the action begins. This helps enormously later on. Be sure the person is close enough to the microphone to be heard.

Remember to tape your graphics! Try taping them all at the beginning, unless you are taping in sequence.

2. EVALUATE THE PRODUCTIONS. Allow time at the end of the session to view what was recorded. Run each tape through completely with pauses, countdowns, mistakes, retakes, and so forth. This is always fun and illuminating.

You may need to schedule another taping session!

Have students informally critique the tapes. Keep comments constructive!

PRODUCTION NOTES:

LESSON 8
LOGGING AND EDITING ROUGH FOOTAGE

TEACHER'S OBJECTIVES

- to help students log their taped scenes.
- to assist students in the effective selection and sequencing of desired scenes.
- to demonstrate effective editing techniques.

STUDENTS' OBJECTIVES

- to correctly log each scene in a videotape.
- to order each scene in the correct sequence to complete a video.

FUNDAMENTALS

Students should have completed their taping. In this session, they will log the takes of each scene—watch the tape and time it or record counter numbers—and select which scenes to put together into a finished video. You should show all students how to log and, if possible, how to edit. You should actually edit, however, with only the producer and director of each video.

Any student in the group can log, but you will find it more efficient to have the producer, director, and/or cameraperson log. It is a good idea to limit the number of students who do the actual editing to these three as well. When decisions have to be made (for example, cutting an entire scene because it is too long or too poorly done), you will want to avoid any personality conflicts or claims of favoritism. Once again, decisions made by the people present at the editing session should be considered final.

Of course, if you want to create the job of editor, now is the chance! Remember to name the editor in the credits. Editing can be tricky. If you know someone in the video field, this may be the time to enlist his or her help. If you taped everything in order, you're done and can go right on to the next lesson.

THE TEACHER WILL NEED TO KNOW

- how to log and edit a videotape. Logging can be simple. Use the Edit Log form in the appendix (p. 88) to note the counter numbers at the beginning and end of each scene. Have students note comments about each scene as they watch, for example, "too loud," "poor lighting," "best shot." Pause after each scene to record this information.

Each video recorder counter works differently, so try to use the same VCR for all the logging. To begin logging, rewind the tape and set the counter at zero. If you rewind a tape you have started to log or stop and try to start over again, your counter numbers may be slightly off. This is normal. (See "Editing," p. 27, for editing procedures.)

STUDENTS WILL NEED TO KNOW

- how to use a VCR to view a tape.
- how to set the counter on the VCR to zero.

MATERIALS

- a VCR for viewing and logging tapes.
- copies of the Edit Log form.
- editing equipment or access to editing equipment or two VCRs.
- blank videotapes to edit onto.

VOCABULARY

Edit

Log

PROCEDURES

Preparation: Inform students that this step produces the finished product. This is where all the hard work pays off.

1. CORRECTLY LOG EACH TAKE OF EACH SCENE. Insert the videotape into the VCR and make sure the VCR counters are at 0000. Give each student an Edit Log form. Explain that the student should record the "in" counter number, the one that the scene begins with, in the left-hand column. The student should record the "out" counter number, the one that the scene ends with, in the second column. In the large right-hand column, the student should note an identifying feature such as an opening line or action that takes place in the scene. Also, ask students to note information about the quality of the scene such as "excellent effect," "poor lighting here," or "car noise too loud." They should star the best take of each scene. (You can now see the value of the countdown before each scene, as well as the "scene 5, take 2" information recorded at the beginning of each take.)

Begin playing the tape and have students log each take of each scene. Stop the tape at intervals and evaluate what you have logged. Which was the best take? Why? Point out subtle differences between takes or problems or even advantages of one over the other. Praise effective takes. Be sure to analyze them for their effectiveness.

After a while you may want to stop logging and leave the rest for your producer/director team. Remind them to rewind the tape and set the counters at 0000 if they start from the beginning (which they must do if the VCR is used by another group and the counter numbers are lost).

2. ORDER THE BEST CHOICE OF EACH SCENE IN THE CORRECT SEQUENCE. Students can manipulate their logging information in several ways to put it in a workable order for editing:

- They can write each logged scene on a slip of paper or index card, complete with all pertinent information such as counter numbers and notes to the editing group ("cut scene after Damien falls" or "need music here"). Cards are particularly helpful because they can be ordered and reordered. They can also be helpful if you are using some takes in another production—you get double duty from them. They can be awkward and easily dropped, however, so be careful if you use this method.

- Students may prefer to jot their order of preference on another sheet. Although much easier to use initially, this can lead to problems later if the sequence must be changed, notes added, and so forth.

Using an appropriate method, students should select the best take of each scene and note these takes in order for the final production. Students should now begin to get some idea of the flow of the final tape. This is also a good time to discuss any problems that can be foreseen with the final production. It is common for students to feel they must retape some scenes or add others. If possible, allow them this luxury. Perhaps you can add extra time into the schedule. Editing takes time, so plan for it.

3. USE EFFECTIVE VIDEO EDITING TECHNIQUES. Show students how to edit using two VCRs. This can produce a passable edit and may be sufficient for your needs at this time.

If you have access to editing equipment, so much the better, although this equipment is usually expensive, and students may need to direct a technician instead of working with the equipment themselves.

In many large cities, video production labs will rent their video editing equipment, but you must use it in their facility. If travel is no problem, you may want to look into this option. Remember your local university or college. The department of teleproduction or media may be willing to let you use their equipment. Investigate your options!

Also inquire whether a community cable corporation has been established to facilitate citizens' involvement in producing video material for public access channels. In many larger cities, such organizations provide equipment free of charge to interested individuals.

When you are finished editing, one important step remains: evaluation.

OPTIONAL ASSIGNMENT
An excellent activity is for the teacher to have a prepared tape of rough footage and ask each student to assemble it into a finished production. To do this, each student will need access to editing equipment. It is also time consuming, so it is best done as homework or as an outside assignment if possible.

LESSON 9
EVALUATION, STUDENT-STYLE

TEACHER'S OBJECTIVES

- to direct students in the evaluation of their video production.
- to evaluate students' productions, performance, and participation.
- to provide feedback to students about their productions, performance, and participation.

STUDENTS' OBJECTIVES

- to recall the Criteria for Evaluation chart from Lesson 1.
- to recall the elements of a video production: theme, setting, plot, mood, characterization, layering.
- to evaluate the completed video productions according to the Criteria for Evaluation chart.

FUNDAMENTALS

After you have had the production party and everyone has watched the videos at least three times, there is one important step that must be accomplished. For maximum growth and learning from this experience, students must evaluate their work. Evaluation forces them to see where they were and what they have done to get where they are now. You will find that some students have already analyzed the productions and have made some rudimentary observations. You need to formalize these comments through class discussion.

Remember Lesson 1? If you wondered why students needed to construct a Criteria for Evaluation chart, now you know. They can finally use their own criteria on themselves. They can become their own critics.

STUDENTS WILL NEED TO

- complete their videos and a Criteria for Evaluation chart from Lesson 1.

MATERIALS

- the Criteria for Evaluation chart created in Lesson 1.
- a chalkboard and chalk.
- a VCR and students' completed tapes.

VOCABULARY

From Lesson 1, review

Characterization

Layering

Mood

Plot

Setting

Theme

PROCEDURES

Preparation: Tell students that they will begin to see and understand their video productions in new ways after today's lesson.

1. RECALL THE ELEMENTS OF A DRAMATIC WORK. Ask students to recall the elements of a dramatic work. Place the elements on the chalkboard as the students name them: theme, setting, plot, mood, characterization, layering. Summarize each element quickly.

2. IDENTIFY THE ELEMENTS OF EACH VIDEO PRODUCTION. Construct a chart on the chalkboard and have the students identify each element for each video. Write each element as it is identified. If students worked in groups, you might want each group to meet and work through these steps.

3. RECALL THE CRITERIA FOR EVALUATION CHART. Ask students to retrieve the Criteria for Evaluation chart they constructed in Lesson 1. Remind students how they applied these criteria to evaluate their favorite television shows.

4. EVALUATE THE VIDEO PRODUCTIONS USING THE CRITERIA FOR EVALUATION. Have students evaluate each video production using their Criteria for Evaluation. You may discover that their criteria need to be updated in light of their experience. Hooray! You might want students to compose a written review of each production according to the Criteria for Evaluation. Make sure every student understands the strengths and weaknesses of each production.

If you find you have a production that is notoriously weak, have that production group analyze their work aloud for the class. Ask them to concentrate on what was effective and what was ineffective. (Questions you might ask: What was the weakest spot in the production? What would have improved the production? What would you keep in the production? Analyze the production in terms of its elements. What have you learned that you can use more effectively in your next production?) This technique is also valuable with a production group that was highly effective. You might want to videotape the analysis of the highly successful group to show in successive years.

Briefly discuss the video productions for their use of layering. Again, stress the point that successful video productions depend on careful thought, preparation, and creativity to structure their effects to the best end. No successful production simply happens. It is planned.

You may want to look at other videos, even the ones you looked at in Lesson 1, to see how student reviews have changed.

APPENDIX

FIG. 1 FIG. 2 FIG. 3

Ways to Use Video in Schools

Optional Lesson: Process Video

Video Production Proposal

Suggestions for Positive Feedback

Materials for the Classroom

Sample Script and
   Storyboard Sheets

Blank Forms
   Script Sheet
   Storyboard Sheet
   Edit Log

Student Skill Chart

Glossary

References

WAYS TO USE VIDEO IN SCHOOLS

Administration

- prepare orientation tapes
- tape student council meetings
- tape sample parent/teacher interviews
- document each year with a "video yearbook"
- use clips from classroom activities at Open House
- share examples of teaching techniques

Art

- demonstrate techniques (close-ups especially valuable)
- tape exhibits to share with other schools or grades
- tape museum tours to share with others
- introduce new art media
- bring local architecture into the classroom
- illustrate perspective, contrast, shadow, and other details

Business

- tape an actual job interview
- demonstrate special techniques (typing, for example)
- demonstrate repair techniques
- interview businesspeople
- tape "on-the-job" documentaries

Driver Training

- demonstrate correct driving techniques
- demonstrate parking, changing a tire, and other activities
- illustrate traffic hazards
- conduct interviews with law personnel, accident victims, and so forth

English

- dramatize stories, myths, plays, poetry
- stage interviews with legendary people
- introduce and demonstrate library techniques
- tape oral readings and presentations for evaluation
- tape students reading books for younger students
- tape students recommending books to younger students

Foreign Language

- tape correct pronunciations and expressions
- tape field trips to plays, countries, cultural events
- tape interviews with people speaking foreign languages
- use animation to demonstrate sounds

General Classroom Teaching

- tape classroom activities for Open House or PTA meetings
- tape special programs to share with class
- document a year's activities for orientation next year
- tape lessons for absent students
- tape introductory lessons to avoid repetition
- tape close-up demonstrations of great detail for general class viewing
- create "commercials" for some aspect of school

Health

- demonstrate first-aid
- analyze proper health areas: posture, nutrition, movement, and so forth
- document incidents of drug or alcohol abuse
- illustrate recognition, prevention, and treatment of disease

Science

- demonstrate scientific methods
- detail experiments, pause to hypothesize results
- document results of experiments
- share science activities with other classes
- document results for science fairs
- share special programs
- illustrate complex, unsafe, or costly experiments

Social Studies

- document field trips
- focus on maps, graphs, diagrams, charts
- dramatize historical events
- record interviews with local resource people
- create "news" programs
- stage interviews

Speech and Theater

- tape student rehearsals
- replay taped performances for evaluation
- document performances
- tape debate techniques
- tape dress rehearsals
- demonstrate physical and audio formation of sounds

Sports

- tape practices for instruction
- tape games or events

OPTIONAL LESSON: PROCESS VIDEO

Teacher's Objectives

- to explain what "process video" is.
- to help students become aware of "video trance."
- to help students make and analyze a process video.

Students' Objectives

- to identify "process video."
- to recognize the viewing habits associated with commercial television and process video.
- to recognize the dangers of "video trance."
- to make a process video and analyze it.

Fundamentals

Process video is different from studio and commercial television in that it is the immediate and direct recording of a live, unrehearsed event. Process video is a window through which we can view how we act with others. Looking at real life events through process video is an important antidote to commercial television, which is often out of touch with reality. No one who has watched commercial television will deny that the video images we see affect our behavior. We respond not only to what we recognize as "information" but to other aspects as well, aspects that we do not always recognize—a fact well known in marketing research. Evidence is increasing, for example, that violence on television teaches us to engage in violent behavior, even though we don't "set out" to learn it.

Process video is used by trainers, professionals, therapists, and others seeking to help people work and relate more effectively. It helps people to see their behavior as others see it and reinforce what is positive and change what is not.

In process video, an event is recorded exactly as it happens. There is no staging, no studio, no prepared script. Process video is straightforward and easy to do. Students can record a school project, a guest presentation, a classroom discussion. Just turn on the camera and roll!

The important part of process video is what happens after the recording. In process video, we see ourselves and others clearly. We see how we act and react with those around us. Process video is an important learning tool. But schooled for years by commercial television, we often must be taught to view process video effectively.

Commercial television strongly influences our viewing habits, not only what we see but how we see it. Our acquired viewing habits frequently interfere with our ability to learn from process video. As a result, it is usually necessary to structure the viewing process so that students can overcome habits acquired through years of viewing commercial television.

Video Trance

The most obvious and serious barrier to learning from process video is "video trance." Watching television is such a passive activity that most people are unprepared to react spontaneously to video material. Most of us watch television as a form of relaxation and we are accustomed to having our attention *drawn* to events rather than *directing* our attention ourselves. We need to actively scan, search, track, and discuss what we see. Commercial television producers, well aware of video trance, attract attention at key points with sounds, music, changes in volume, flashes, crashes, sexual imagery, unexpected events, visual distortions, and a variety of other techniques. As a result, many viewers face the television or video monitor and expect to be spoon-fed.

Breaking Barriers to Learning

Do not be discouraged if students seem disinterested or unwilling to invest any energy in learning from process video. You are probably seeing the overt signs of video trance. You can disrupt it in several ways:

Identify the Problem. Before beginning to study process video, describe video trance. Many students are better able to maintain their vigilance once they are aware of the problem.

Break It Up. The attention span for this kind of video material runs between five and ten minutes for untrained viewers. Keep it short and you'll keep your audience. Most process videos are not viewed from start to finish. A segment is often preselected to stimulate discussion.

Guide Discussion. Briefly tell students what they will see in the preselected video segment. Because commercial television highlights the "message" so clearly, most viewers are not prepared to absorb all the information in a video. Direct students' attention to significant details. If possible, stand beside the monitor and point out important events. A remote control device is almost essential for viewing process video effectively. Help students *scan* the total picture. Events in the background may be just as relevant as events in the foreground. Ask students to *search* the total picture for important events. Have students *track* important people and activities. A videographer cannot always follow a significant activity and keep it in focus. Tracking is the ability to follow people or activities even though they move about in the picture, come in and out of focus, or recede into the background. Help students track important people or events by standing beside the monitor and pointing.

Discussion. You can reduce the passivity of video trance by talking about the video material segment by segment. Ask students to comment on what they see. Many such comments are critical. Ask students for alternative approaches and ideas. Viewers learn from the discussion as well as from the video. In many learning situations, the video is used mainly to stimulate discussion prior to solving a problem or making a decision. Discussion also lets you measure what students are getting from the tape—can they observe accurately and reconstruct events that they have seen?

Repeat It. Use your remote control (or search dial if your machine has one) to repeat and review material. Fast forwarding or rewinding allows students to immediately review certain segments.

Substance vs. Appearance

Commercial television is partially responsible for our fixation on appearance—clothing, hair, makeup. When you see yourself on video for the first time, it is typical to get caught up in your appearance. It helps to talk about this phenomenon in advance and discuss with your students what process video is really all about—substance. We are not looking at how we appear. We are looking at how we behave, particularly in collaboration with others.

THE TEACHER WILL NEED TO KNOW

- what process video is.

MATERIALS

- a short process video (for example, a tape of a classroom discussion).
- a taped television commercial.
- a VCR and television.
- a remote control device for the VCR.

VOCABULARY

Process video

Scan

Search

Track

Video trance

PROCEDURES

Preparation: Ask students if they ever got so involved in a televison program that they failed to hear or see things around them. After students share their experiences, discuss the advantages and disadvantages of this behavior. Explain that today's lesson will give them new ways to deal with this experience.

1. DEFINE VIDEO TRANCE.
Ask students to describe their experience with video trance. Tell them that in contrast to commercial television, process video is like looking through a window at how we learn. (We're teaching and learning all the time, although it's not formally recognized.)

2. TELEVISION VS. PROCESS VIDEO.
Review a segment of a rental movie, television show, or television commercial for the techniques used to attract our attention. Ask students to contrast these segments with real life. Have students make a list of these comparisons. For example, do police shoot their guns every day? Most do only a few times in their career.

3. REVIEW PROCESS VIDEO.
Review with students the process video you have made. Guide their observation. Use the vocabulary "scan," "search," and "track." Have them discuss what they see.

4. VIDEO A SCHOOL PROJECT.
If you do not have a process videotape, ask students to tape a school project to learn more about process. Or give students the camera and have them tape you teaching the class or "peer helper" activities, one student helping another on some project. The idea is for the camera to look at the teaching and the learning to discover which methods work and which do not. Encourage students to review the tapes and scan, search, track, and discuss. Tape the same activity on another day and discuss it again.

5. VIDEO A STUDENT DISCUSSION.
Have students tape their discussion of a process video segment and then review the discussion. Always remember that the focus is on learning and finding out what methods are most effective. Remind students that this is the goal of process video. For example,
"Look, Mark's beginning to share his ideas in discussion. And Joanne is listening more and letting others talk. Steve gave a nice explanation of where the nurse is to that new student." Discussions of process video should always have a positive focus.

6. EVALUATE YOUR PROCESS VIDEO SESSION.
Ask students what they have learned about process video. Ask for new examples of how students could use process video.

7. HOMEWORK.
For extra credit, students can take home a process video segment and share it with their parents.

8. SHARE IT WITH THE PRINCIPAL.
Have students share a process video with the principal. Have students do a trial run with you first. Help them design their presentation. You could even videotape it.

9. PROCESS VIDEO IN THE SCHOOL.
Let it be known that your class is available to make process videotapes to be used in school. Have them practice presenting the finished process video to the people involved and guiding discussion.

VIDEO PRODUCTION PROPOSAL

Complete each section thoroughly and have your proposal approved by your teacher before you begin production. Use another sheet of paper if necessary.

I. Statement of Purpose of the Production.
What is the purpose of this video? What is it you want the viewer to have after seeing your video that he or she didn't have before? What will be your point of view?

II. Analyze the Intended Audience.
Describe a single member of your audience as thoroughly as possible. Think about age, sex, educational level, socioeconomic status, and so forth. This will help you with Section I above and will provide a solid basis for developing the remaining steps.

III. Summary of Content.
Break down the video into scenes and state what will be covered in each scene.

IV. Production Format.

What kind of video will this be—an educational, documentary, humorous, or dramatic one?

A. Summarize in a short paragraph the intended plot of your video. Include a description of setting and mood.

B. List by character name each character in the script, along with a short description of that character's physical appearance and personality.

C. What materials do you need for your video: audio (sound), staging (set), lighting, graphics, or special props? Include a complete script and storyboard and a floor plan of the set if necessary.

V. Budget.

Consider your needs for materials, space, equipment, and people. Submit as real a budget as possible. Talk to your teacher about what the school can provide.

VI. Evaluation.

What recommendations do you have for measuring the success of your video with your intended audience?

This Video Production Proposal is due before you begin production. It will be evaluated on originality, creativity, and practicality as well as on quality of thought, neatness, spelling, grammar, and promptness. It can be typed or printed neatly.

SUGGESTIONS FOR POSITIVE FEEDBACK

p. 19

A sample statement of praise. "Look how Diane really had a sense for color in this shot—the way the straw flowers and the child's hair look together."

p. 44

"It was teamwork that paid off here—your director, Marcia, cued Rob the cameraperson to go to the medium shot and give Barbara the guest more looking room—see how the shot is balanced now?"

p. 45

"Let's look for the spot where Steve changes the frame—notice any difference? Does this work better?"

p. 48

Regarding brainstorming, encourage participation. Help the group avoid judgment and avoid discussion of brainstormed ideas for the moment. "It looks like Mark wants to say something. What's your idea?"

p. 49

Be firm about more thought in simplistic videos. "Yes, we see violence on TV a lot. What we're after here are *your* ideas about what stories you want to tell with video. What do you like doing yourself? Our video project is for your new ideas. Try to do something we haven't seen done before. What stories in real life have meant the most to you?"

p. 69

"Let's find out more about the planning that went into this effective piece. George's team revised their production plan several times before they were satisfied with it. Remember their great scene under the bleachers? That was an idea that came up only after they taped how they originally planned it. This group was not afraid to make changes to make their piece better. Also, it was Sarah the cameraperson's idea for the bleacher shot and her director Melissa was receptive to it."

MATERIALS FOR THE CLASSROOM

Graphics

The art resource teacher in your school can be a wonderful source of information for ways and means of producing graphics for your video production. Consult him or her with technical questions about materials and media, how to use various adhesives, and how to choose color for maximum impact. If your school has an art room, perhaps arrangements could be made to use it as working space for creating graphics. If some of your students are artistically inclined, perhaps they could work with the art teacher. Be sure to arrange for using the space and get permission to use tools and materials!

A visit to your local art or office supply store will give you a wide choice of materials and methods for producing type. Commercially produced press-on and pressure-sensitive letters are available in many typestyles, sizes, colors, and materials. Some are removable and some are permanent. Many art suppliers offer a catalog of available typestyles that makes a good reference for your class-room. You can also make enlarged photocopies of pages from these catalogs and cut and paste the letters on white paper.

If you have access to a computer either in your home or at school, consider using computer-generated typesetting. Many programs are available that allow you to set up an entire page with the letters exactly where you want them in the frame (centered or lined up on the left with plenty of white space around the edges). Some computers allow a wide choice of typestyles and weights, with many options for layout and even graphics (like the one that produced this book!). Some photocopy outlets offer self-serve computer time, with high quality laser output, at a reasonable cost. Explore all your options. Consult the resource people at your school, and don't forget the parents!

Making Transparencies

Using pages from this book, other written materials, or graphics, it is easy to make transparencies to display on an overhead projector. At least four options are available:

1. Place clear acetate (available from art and office supply stores) over the material to be copied and trace it using special pens for making overhead transparencies or permanent markers. They come in a variety of colors and will not rub off.

2. Use the Thermofax machine at your school with a special clear base instead of the standard "ditto" master. Ask your teacher's aide or instructional resource person for help.

3. Use the photocopy machine at your school with special clear acetate (it replaces the paper in the paper tray), available through district supply or your office supply store.

4. Your local photocopy shop will make transparencies for you at a reasonable price.

Mask out areas you don't want to copy with white paper. This enables you to copy only one section of a page or eliminate a page number.

Most photocopy machines now enlarge and reduce, allowing you to be creative with your transparencies!

SAMPLE SCRIPT AND STORYBOARD SHEETS

Video Column Suggestions

- Place camera directions in the video column, spaced alongside the audio directions.
- Use ALL CAPITAL LETTERS and single spacing in camera directions.
- Use quotation marks and upper- and lower-case letters for titles and graphics.
- Leave several lines of space between video descriptions.

Audio Column Suggestions

- Identify the speaker for all spoken lines when beginning each speech and after each interruption.
- Use underlined capital letters for the speaker. Put the name on a line by itself with a colon.
- Use capital and lower-case letters for words to be spoken.
- Indicate voice-overs or narrations with parentheses.
- Directions to talent—on or off camera—appear in the audio column.
- Sound cues are separate from speech.

SCRIPT SHEET

VIDEO	AUDIO
FADE IN	**HOST:** Welcome to A.M. People. I'm Linda Hostess and with me today is Samson Smith, a new student in our class.
ZOOM OUT TO 2 SHOT OF HOST AND GUEST	TELL ME, Samson, what do you like most about our class, what do you do in our class, and what encouraged you to say "yes" to being in video production?
CU OF GUEST	**GUEST:** In video production we do interesting things. We work with cameras and equipment. We learn to do video in an exciting way. We do it ourselves! I like that!
2 SHOT OF HOST AND GUEST	**HOST:** Okay, I think you've answered most of my questions. Audience, if you have any questions, please call 1-800-V-I-D-E-O. Thank you for coming, Samson.
ZOOM IN TO CU OF HOST	And thank you for watching. Stay with us, because after this commercial we'll interview Wally The Gorilla.
FADE TO BLACK	

Producer _____

Producer/Director_____

FADE IN

Zoom OUT TO 2 SHOT of (H)+(G)

CU of GUEST

AUDIO **HOST:** Welcome to A.M. People. I'm Linda Hostess and with me today is Samson Smith, a new student in our class.

AUDIO **H:** tell me, Samson, what do you like about our class, what do you do in our class and what encouraged you to say "yes" to being in video production?

AUDIO **GUEST:** IN video production we do interesting things. We work with cameras and equipment. We learn to do video in an exciting way: We do it ourselves! I like that.

2 SHOT of (H)+(G)

ZOOM IN TO CU of (H)

FADE TO BLACK

AUDIO **H:** Okay, I think you've answered most of my questions. Audience, if you have any questions, please call 1-800-V-I-D-E-O. Thank you for coming, Samson.

AUDIO **H:** AND THANK you for watching. Stay with us, because after this commercial we'll interview Wally the Gorilla

AUDIO

BLANK FORMS

Script Sheet
Storyboard Sheet
Edit Log

SCRIPT SHEET

Program _____
Producer/Director _____

VIDEO	AUDIO

STORYBOARD SHEET

Program_____

Producer/Director_____

Audio

Audio

Audio

Audio

Audio

Audio

EDIT LOG

Counter Number		Audio/Video Cue		
		IN		OUT

STUDENT SKILL CHART

Students should acquire the following skills at each stage of video production:

Preproduction
- Identify theme, plot, setting, characterizations, mood
- Analyze these elements for relationships
- Construct character analyses

Production
- Operate camera: on/off, record/pause, zoom in/out, pan, tilt, dolly, truck
- Execute camera shots: ECU, CU, MS, LS
- Frame shots: use rule of thirds, place subject's eyes two-thirds of the way up screen, allow for "head" room and "talking space"
- Directing cues and gestures: "stand by," "roll tape," prompting "5-4-3-2-1," "action," countdown at end of scene "5-4-3-2-1-cut!"
- Use constructive feedback to guide talent and crew during scenes

Postproduction
- Log tapes
- Structure scenes into appropriate sequence for finished video
- Edit scenes into appropriate sequence
- Evaluate finished video

Peripherals
Graphics
- Plan and construct simple graphics
- Use prepared graphics
- Construct simple graphics according to plans
- Plan and construct special effects graphics

Lights
- Create and use simple lighting plans
- Create and use special effects lighting

Sound
- Use given sound equipment
- Create and use simple audio plans
- Create and use special audio effects

Costumes/Set
- Create and use simple costumes and set designs
- Create and use special effects in costumes and set designs

GLOSSARY

Audience: everyone who will view a particular videotape

Audio: the sound portion of a videotape, usually found on two tracks

Audio dub: to record sound only, without disturbing the picture portion of a videotape; sometimes audio can be dubbed on one track only, preserving the original sound on the other track

Audio head: the magnetic recording head that records or plays back sound

Audio in: a sound input connection for incoming sound signals

Audio out: a sound output connection for outgoing sound signals

Back light: on a video set, a light coming from behind the subject

Bouncing light: a technique that uses a white surface to reflect light to fill in harsh shadows

Cable: a wire carrying video and/or audio signals from one piece of equipment to another

Camcorder: a video camera that records directly onto an inserted videotape

Characterizations: the physical and psychological profiles of the characters

Close-up (CU): a camera shot in which an object or part of an object is seen at close range or framed tightly

Criteria: the standards on which a judgment is based

"Cut": the director's cue to stop the recording

Director: in a video production, the person responsible for the script, storyboard, camera shots, and all other day-to-day activities

Documentary: a video treatment that presents a subject for historical purposes

Dolly in or out: to physically move the whole camera forward or back; also, the wheeled frame onto which a tripod fits

Dramatic: a video treatment that dramatizes some fictional or nonfictional story

Dub: to copy all or part of a video program from one videotape to another

Edit: to select and electronically assemble two or more audio and video segments into a single program

Educational: a video treatment that demonstrates how something works, presents factual information, or describes something

Extreme close-up (ECU): a very close camera shot

Fade: in audio, to decrease in volume; in video, to make the picture go gradually black ("fade out") or appear gradually on screen from black ("fade in")

Fill light: on a video set, an artificial light used to fill in shadows

Focal length: the distance between the camera lens and the recording surface

Focus: the sharpness and clarity of the picture

Generation loss: the successive reduction of video quality that occurs during dubbing

Graphics: any written or drawn material used on camera

Head: the electromagnetic device that records or retrieves information from magnetic tape

Head room: the space between the top of the screen and the object in the frame

Humorous: a video treatment that seeks to make people laugh

Jump cut: when a picture obviously skips from shot to shot or skips intermediate action

Key spot: on a video set, the main light

Layering: in constructing a video, the deliberate choice of varying elements to appeal to a variety of audiences

Lens: an optical lens, necessary for perceiving an image

Line in: an audio or video input point from other equipment

Line out: an audio or video output point to other equipment

Lip sync: when the picture of a person's lips moving matches the sound of his or her voice

Log: to watch a videotape and make an inventory of the various recorded scenes on it

Long shot (LS): a camera shot that includes a large field of view

Medium shot (MS): a camera shot that shows a person from the waist up or about half an object and some background

Monitor/receiver: a dual-function standard television receiver and monitor that both receives and transmits audio and video signals

Mood: the tone of the production, such as humorous, dramatic, fantastic, or introspective

Pan: to pivot the camera from side to side

Plot: the storyline of the work

Point of view: the perspective taken in a video production

Postproduction: usually refers to the editing process

Preproduction: the planning stage of any production (includes script writing, research, scheduling, and budget planning)

Process video: videotaping that records a "process" or live, unrehearsed action

Producer: in a video production, the person responsible for the content, audience, and objectives of the production

Ready cue: the director's signal to talent and crew that taping is imminent

"Roll tape": the director's cue for the cameraperson to begin recording

Roll time: the 5-count interval in which the videotape is rolling but the action has not yet begun

Scan: in viewing process video, to review the video frame quickly for important elements in both the foreground and background

Scoop light: inexpensive clip-on lights with a single bulb and metal casing

Search: in viewing process video, to discover important people or events in each frame

Setting: the location in place and time in which the work occurs

Special effects: transitional effects (such as wipes, fades, or dissolves) or complementary effects (such as titles); also describes digitally produced effects (such as picture flips)

"Stand by": the director's cue that videotaping is imminent

Studio video: videotaping that occurs in a controlled studio setting

Sync: shortened form of synchronization, the timing pulses that keep television scanning circuits working together

Take: the recording of a single shot or scene

Talent: in a video production, the people who appear on camera

"Tape rolling": the cameraperson's response to tell the director that videotape recording has begun

Teamwork: in a video production, the result of all crewmembers respecting the hierarchy of authority and working together effectively

Theme: the overall idea for a work

Tilt: a camera shot that points the camera up or down

Time Cues "5,4,3,2,1": the director's cues that the action will begin in 5 counts

Titles: any graphic material shown on camera

Track: in viewing process video, to follow important people or events throughout the entire videotape

Tracking: an electronic alignment of the video heads so that what is played back matches what was recorded, giving a clearer picture

Treatment: the manner in which the subject of a video production is portrayed

Truck: to physically move the camera left or right to follow the subject

Two-shot: framing two people or objects with the camera lens

Video: the picture portion of a videotape

Video in: a video input point from other equipment

Video out: a video output point to other equipment

Video trance: the passive manner in which most people have learned to watch commercial television

Videotape: magnetic tape that can record a television signal

"You're on" (action): the director's cue to talent to begin the action

Zoom: the gradual changing of the focal length of the lens, giving the effect of dollying without moving the camera, accomplished by pressing the camera's zoom toggle button

Zoom in: using the lens to give the effect of moving closer to the subject

Zoom out: using the lens to give the effect of moving away from the subject